The Barefoot Anthropologist

The Highlands of Champa and Vietnam in the Words of Jacques Dournes

Andrew Hardy

ÉCOLE FRANÇAISE D'EXTRÊME-ORIENT

PARIS

Silkworm Books

CHIANG MAI

The EFEO–Silkworm Books Series is an innovative collaboration between the École Française d'Extrême-Orient (EFEO) and Silkworm Books, initiated in 2011, to bring outstanding EFEO research on Asia to a wider readership.

Cover photos and all other photos, except the photo of the author, courtesy of Missions étrangères de Paris

A Vietnamese edition of this book was published by Nxb Tri Thức as part of the EFEO Trails of History Series, under the title *Nhà nhân học chân trần: Nghe và đọc Jacques Dournes* (Hanoi, 2013).

First published in 2015 by
Silkworm Books
6 Sukkasem Road, T. Suthep
Chiang Mai 50200 Thailand
info@silkwormbooks.com
www.silkwormbooks.com

Typeset in Arno Pro 11 pt. by Silk Type

If one hasn't been barefoot in the paddy field, one knows nothing, because everything happens in people's heads.

What interests me is people in relation to their milieu: what they do with it, what they make of it, diachronically, through the centuries and through the evolution of people's politics and psychology—how people, barefoot in the paddy fields with mud halfway up their legs, reflect, react, think, and dream of other things.

—Jacques Dournes
Bagard, February 1992

Contents

Part 1
Jacques Dournes, Highland Champa, and the Potao:
Reading Pötao, une théorie du pouvoir chez les Indochinois jörai
15

Part 2
The Vietnamese and Highlanders in the Twentieth Century:
Interview with Jacques Dournes
63

Afterword
Barefoot in the Mud: Reflections on Jacques Dournes
Oscar Salemink
93

Appendix
French Transcript of the Interview with
Jacques Dournes
99

Foreword

In the early years of this twenty-first century, while studying and collecting epic poems in the Central Highlands of Vietnam, I had not yet had the chance to read many documents written by French authors about the region because very few had been translated into Vietnamese. The researchers of the previous generation knew French and the books they wrote reflected their reading of French materials. The extent of their understanding probably varied, but at least the names of French scholars who worked on Vietnam are mentioned in their works. However, there is a limit to the knowledge that can be obtained through such reading. What those French scholars' work was like, what issues they addressed, what ideologies and messages they wanted to convey, what their experiences and methodologies were—these remained as questions in the minds of the Vietnamese scholars who do not read French.

So it is a matter for celebration that, thanks to the EFEO and several overseas funding agencies in Vietnam, many French monographs have been translated into Vietnamese. Vietnamese readers now have direct access to well-known works and authors. Among those works, I should mention those written about the Central Highlands. They have received particular attention, partly because of their intrinsic interest and partly because current events in that region have never been taken lightly. At the same time it is true to say that, despite their translation by people with a deep knowledge of French and of the authors and works translated, reading those works is very challenging. This is understandable, in the light of their authors' circumstances, experiences, and scholarship, as well as their use of field data, which are all quite different from those of today.

The fact remains that these books are not easy to read, and this is all the more true of the works of Jacques Dournes.

I learned a great deal about Jacques Dournes from Father Nguyễn Huy Trọng, a priest at the parish church of Kala, at Di Linh in Lâm Đồng province, whom I met in late 2001 (to be precise, on December 12, 2001). Father Trọng said that this was where Jacques Dournes lived for six years before he moved to Kon Tum, and it was here that he wrote the Koho–French dictionary and his study of the Mạ people's customary law (N'dri). Later on (in May 2002), I returned to interview Father Trọng, who ran the church after Dournes left. Whenever mention was made of his predecessor and the time he spent here, the priest expressed his deep respect and admiration for him.

I was fortunate to represent the Institute of Culture (Vietnam Academy of Social Sciences) as a member of the scientific committee that worked with the EFEO on the Vietnamese translation of Dournes's *Pötao, une théorie de pouvoir chez les Indochinois jörai* (published in Hanoi by EFEO and Nxb Tri Thức in 2011). Andrew Hardy and I co-wrote the book's preface. Like many other readers, I found understanding Dournes and his work extremely difficult. But the book exudes his passion and love for the people and land of the Central Highlands, where he used to live. In turn, that passion explains why he did not want to be far from the highlanders and was ready to abandon everything he had, even his home country, to live with them. Historical circumstances, however, did not allow him to fulfill this wish and forced him to return to France, causing him much pain and sadness.

After he returned to France, we are lucky that someone went to seek his advice, asked him to share some of the ideas that he had not had the time or the inclination to write down, took an interest in his viewpoint, spent time with him, and was able to "put up with" him. That someone was Andrew Hardy. The result of his visit is this book, *The Barefoot Anthropologist: The Highlands of Champa and Vietnam in the Words of Jacques Dournes*.

In my view, this is not just a book of poignant reminiscences through which Dournes relates the stresses he labored under. It is also a precious record offering a deeper understanding of him and his work and, most importantly, contains a collection of "kitchen stories" of immense methodological value. Andrew Hardy's contribution is to help Jacques Dournes continue leaving his footprints in the "mud" of the Central Highlands after he is no longer able to go there himself, and to connect those footprints to scholars of the Central Highlands of the present and future generations.

Lê Hồng Lý
Institute of Culture
Vietnam Academy of Social Sciences

Acknowledgments

I would like to thank the following colleagues, whose comments helped improve the completed work: François Lagirarde, Gérard Fouquet, Jérémy Jammes, Charlotte Minh Ha Pham, Patrizia Zolese. I would like to express my gratitude to Oscar Salemink for his afterword. Oscar also greatly improved the book as a whole by giving the manuscript several critical readings and contributing much highly valuable advice. The book's failings are my responsibility alone.

My thanks go to the Société des Missions Étrangères de Paris (MEP), for permission to reproduce the photographs published in this volume, and to Father Gérard Moussay and Ghislaine Olive for their help with my research in the MEP archives. Thanks to Trịnh Anh Tú for the photo of lunch in Ba Tơ.

Thanks also to the editors of *Aséanie*, where an edited and condensed version of my interview with Dournes was published in December 2009 (number 24) under the title "Le XXe siècle chez les Montagnards et les Vietnamiens, raconté par Jacques Dournes à Andrew Hardy (Bagard, France—1er et 2 février 1992)." The English transcript in part 2 is a translation of this version. A fuller version of the interview is presented in French in the appendix. My thanks to Pascaline Mariette and Clémence Le Meur for proofreading the French text.

It is always a pleasure working with Lê Hồng Lý and his colleagues at the Institute of Culture in Hanoi. Nguyên Ngọc's help has also been invaluable.

Thanks as usual go to Vũ Thị Mai Anh.

I am grateful to Béa Narcy and Marguerita Young, who introduced me to Jacques Dournes.

Introduction

Jacques Dournes arrived in Vietnam in 1946 as a young Catholic missionary from France. He so thoroughly identified with the villagers of the Central Highlands among whom he settled that they soon became his people and his adopted home. He was a keen observer of highland society, and by the time he returned to his country of origin a quarter of a century later, he had become a seasoned ethnographer. Back in France he completed formal anthropological studies and produced much valuable scholarship on the highlanders of Vietnam. He became well known for his opinionated and immoderate discourse, arising, in turn, out of his deep passion for his adopted people and his deep alienation from his own society.

This presentation of Dournes's written and spoken words takes two quite different forms. The first is a study based on my multiple readings of his 1977 book on the Potao, the kings of fire, water, and wind, a religious institution in Vietnam's Central Highlands that underpinned the social and political organization of the Jarai ethnic group.[1] The second is an edited transcript of my interview with Dournes, recorded in 1992. Part 1 makes accessible a difficult text written within the structuralist strand of anthropology and addresses a number of questions about the Central Highlands at the time of Champa. Part 2 presents a conversational overview of the history of Vietnam and the Central Highlands in the twentieth century.

In addition to presenting the words of Dournes, the book has two secondary aims. The first is to highlight and develop certain aspects of

---

1. Dournes used the spelling Jörai for this ethnonym. I use the conventional English spelling Jarai (Vietnamese Gia rai) and generally follow the Vietnamese government in spelling the names of other ethnic groups.

Dournes's life, thought, and research regarding the highlanders with whom he lived for twenty-five years, and also regarding Champa and Vietnam. This account is begun in part 1 and narrated more fully by Dournes himself in part 2. Secondly, the book portrays the efforts of a younger researcher entering a new field of study. I knew little about Vietnam when I met Dournes in 1992 and I knew even less about Champa in 2004, when I started reading his book *Pötao*. I hope that the narrative presented in part 1 of these first steps in a research journey—of the evolution of a process of thought—will be helpful to readers embarking on similar projects.

Part 1 Dournes's *Pötao, une théorie du pouvoir*

Dournes once said that the best book ever written on Vietnam's Central Highlands was Maitre's *Les jungles moï*, published in 1912.[2] One hundred years later, my own list of best books has two titles: Maitre's classic study and Dournes's *Pötao, une théorie du pouvoir*.[3] Dournes's years in the hills gave him deep insights into highlander civilization and, in particular, into the meaning and functioning of politics in this society notable for the absence of a state apparatus. The complexity of the subject is, however, compounded by several other difficulties presented by the book. It is a highly structured text, written in concentric circles mirroring Dournes's understanding of Jarai cosmology, each drawing on data gathered with a different methodology. Historical documents are treated in the early chapters, while myths, legends, and other ethnographic material are subjected to structuralist analysis in the later sections. For those who have yet to develop a taste for structuralism, reading *Pötao, une théorie du pouvoir* is not easy.

---

2. Personal communication from Oscar Salemink. Dournes made the remark to Salemink during the 1980s. In his unpublished "Sabre et Bouclier," Dournes commented on Henri Maitre and his book *Les jungles moïs*: "He was a pugnacious and patriotic ethnographer who knew how to observe, and he learned a great deal. This resulted in the most valuable, cited, and pillaged book of the early part of the century" (Ethnographe baroudeur et patriote, sachant observer, [il] a beaucoup appris : il en est résulté l'ouvrage le plus valable, cité et pillé du début de ce siècle).

3. The translated English title is *Potao, a theory of power*.

To render the book more accessible, I have applied the knowledge it contains to a specific research problem: the presence of ancient Champa in its mountainous hinterland, known in Vietnamese today as Tây Nguyên. *Le haut Champa*, or upper Champa, a historical term for the highlands coined by Dournes, and the relationship of the Jarai with the Cham preoccupied Dournes for many years. He wrote an article specifically on the subject[4] and it emerges in many of his other works, including *Pötao, une théorie du pouvoir*. The theme can also be found in a collage of his photographs of the Jarai people, entitled *Pays Jörai*, which he compiled and annotated but never published.[5] This was the subject I was studying while reading the book and I learned a great deal from Dournes's analysis. My indirect approach to the book *Pötao, une théorie du pouvoir* also underlines the point that this, like other texts, bears multiple readings, which depend on the questions brought to it by the reader.

Part 2 Interview with Dournes

A more direct approach is used in part 2, which presents the transcript of my 1992 interview with Dournes. The interview has been substantially cut and is now half as long as the original. The editing had two aims: removal of verbal "noise" and chitchat normal in conversation but distracting to read, and removal of passages irrelevant to the main subjects discussed. The readers' attention is thus drawn to three topics. The first is the twentieth-century history of Vietnam, notably the period after 1946 when Dournes lived there. The second is the economic history of Vietnam and the Central Highlands. The third is the idea of economy (*les sous*) in opposition to that of culture (*le gratuit*), drawing on Dournes's research among the highlanders. Some of Dournes's digressions shed light on his life, character, and literary tastes and have been retained in the untranslated transcript, published here in the appendix.

My light editorial approach means that some critical work is required from the reader. Dournes's views were often extreme, sometimes violent,

---

4. Dournes, "Recherches sur le haut Champa."
5. Dournes, *Pays Jörai* (Hanoi: EFEO/Nxb Tri Thức, forthcoming).

and, from time to time, historically inaccurate. They were frequently couched in abusive language, a symptom of the severance of his ties to society. This was not only a result of his retirement to the isolated country cottage where I met him in southern France. Early in his life, he made a conscious choice to live deracinated in a distant land. In the first minutes of a documentary filmed in 1990, he spoke of his desire as a young man to separate himself from his family and from France: "The less I was home, the better it suited me. . . . I did not want to go mad. I had to leave! After thinking about the Missionary Society, I wanted to go to Asia—because it's the farthest, it's the farthest possible, because it's the most difficult."[6] Once there, he immersed himself—*enraciné*—among the highlanders. "*Mes moïs*" he called them, and the deep affection with which he used the term emptied it of its usual pejorative meaning. During his Vietnam years, he remained outside of the social mainstream: "I was in my shell . . . I was exclusively a minorities guy."[7] His return to Paris after 1970 was not a social success, although it was during this period that he published his finest anthropological work.

He directed boundless scorn at those who remained in the world he had abandoned. Within academia, few colleagues were spared (the footnotes to *Pötao* are particularly revealing in this respect). During the interview, entire disciplines were dismissed: geography, sociology, economics, even ethnology itself. "*Allergique*" to the very word *economy*, he despised every political system on his horizon: Pétain's Vichy regime; France's fourth and fifth republics and its 1990s government; Russian communism; Vietnamese communism; American anti-communism; Vietnam's Bảo Đại regime (1949–55); and the Republic of Vietnam in the South (1955–75). He was deeply "anti-development." This rejection encompassed the development models applied in Vietnam by both regimes (Hanoi and

---

6. "*Moins j'étais chez moi, plus ça m'allait.... Je ne voulais pas devenir fou, il faut sortir ! J'ai commencé par préparer l'École navale, pour partir !... Quand j'ai pensé aux Missions, je voulais l'Asie—parce que c'est plus loin, c'est le plus loin possible, parce que c'est plus difficile.*" Choron-Baix, L'homme des Jörai.

7. All the unreferenced citations here are from my recorded interview with Dournes. Most may be found transcribed in part 2.

Saigon) and elsewhere by communist Russia and capitalist France and America. He extended his contempt even into ancient history, comparing the grocers of Rome unfavorably to the tragedians of Athens.

A few personalities nonetheless merited his respect—Claude Lévi-Strauss, Ho Chi Minh. A handful of literary figures won his praise—Graham Greene, George Orwell, Alain Resnais. His love-hate relationship with the work of Marguerite Duras is revealing of the critical mind he brought to his literary tastes but also of his overly emotional reaction to a disappointing read.

His historical observations are at times contrary to the record. He tried to persuade me that French rule in Vietnam "wasn't as terrible as all that," that there were no "horrible scenes," that it had left "very good memories." He maintained that plantation laborers in the highlands were not unhappy, and that the population of colonial Vietnam knew no hunger. On these points, the historical evidence is against him.

Others of his views are debatable. At one point, he refused to let me call the Franco-Vietnamese conflict of 1946–54 a war. "It was comedy," he finally concluded. If we are to believe him, Vietnam was inhabited at that time by some French busy making money, while other French cowered in remote forts in fear of a paltry threat from the Viet Minh ("skirmishes in the bush"). This is not entirely untrue. But it is certainly not the whole story. It is a partial perspective on a period when all Vietnamese who supported and opposed the Viet Minh knew very well that their country was at war. Likewise we should understand his view of the French colonialists' respect for the land of Vietnam ("they destroyed nothing") in its context as a rhetorical device, spoken to contrast with Vietnam's policies in the highlands and America's policies in Indochina. On several occasions, he contradicted himself, sometimes with rhetorical intent but sometimes not. Were there thieves among the Jarai or not? Were the highlands the "calmest country in the world" or not? Elsewhere, he likened the Vietnamese to the highlanders: "culturally completely different, but psychologically they are small farmers of small plots of land." Once again, to this I would now reply, "Well, yes, but also no."

Above all, he romanticized the highlanders. This is most clear in his remarks on their justice system. "They sing, they recite, singing verses: 'If there is this, there is that—if there is that, there is this, etc., etc.' It goes on for hours. It's so beautiful that in the end everyone says okay and the dispute is settled. It's over. No one says any more about it—no prison, no judge, no fine, no debt, nothing. They have a good drink and it's over." Perhaps this was true in the 1960s, when the village system of customary law was already limited by the presence of a state system in the highlands. A century earlier, however, things had been very different. I cannot believe that Dournes had forgotten the contents of Dourisboure's book, with its accounts of trials by egg and trials by water, of internecine raids and the sale of prisoners into slavery. I simply do not believe that he did not know the highlanders had practiced a judicial system of fines, servitude, and exile.[8] In this respect, he took a position in opposition to the realities he knew, and in a certain sense to history itself; he wanted to stop the clock.

"Dournes has his point of view." A Paris academic dismissed Dournes with these words when I mentioned my visit in 1992. But the same words—if we may strip them of their pejorative overtones—offer us a way to read the transcript of my conversation with Dournes. During the weekend I spent at his house, his views formed a panorama of Vietnam's twentieth-century history and the story of the Central Highlands. His perspective was that of a man who had lived an unusual life during this transitional period and had developed a unique way of thinking about what he saw and experienced. These were things, as he himself said, "I know completely, from every side: the French side, the Vietnamese side, the minorities' side." The same is true of his theoretical ideas: they were formed during long years in the field. This, I believe, is the main value of the transcript.

His account contains flashes of profound insight. He realized that Vietnamese Confucianism concealed a reality of economically autonomous villages ("it is relatively anarchic: there is no higher power, everyone gets by in their corner"). He then saw that this was a factor in

8. Dourisboure, *Les sauvages Ba-Hnars*, 200, 424–29.

the victory of Vietnamese communism ("it finds dots everywhere on the map where its troops can be resupplied"). He likewise understood the Vietnamese aversion to trees ("the Vietnamese are market gardeners—rice growers and market gardeners: sweep it all away, all clean, all clear") and their obsession with immediate returns on investment. This, he recognized, had contributed to the failure of organized migration to the highlands after 1975 and thus to the departure of the boat people. Many of the boat refugees were not fleeing communism as such; they were former participants on an unworkable resettlement program who had nowhere else to go.

During the interview, he explained his idea of "*la comédie*," as it applied to his own, highly performative speech. "I have a strong voice" (*j'ai de la voix*), he rightly boasted. In my editing choices, I have attempted to strike a balance between respect for this extraordinary voice and the need to produce a focused and readable text. In part 2, my translation of the transcript is an edited and condensed version that draws attention to Dournes's ideas. Meanwhile, the longer French version in the appendix gives full rein to the anthropologist's voice. Here, only the lengthier digressions in the original recording have been cut, along with many insults directed at both living and departed individuals. I have not otherwise found it necessary to censure or annotate Dournes's views. It was his idea that I should bring a voice recorder for the weekend I spent with him. I hope this text is adequate homage to that generous and prescient idea.

Jacques Dournes, Highland Champa, and the Potao: Reading *Pötao, une théorie du pouvoir chez les Indochinois jörai*[1]

Jacques Dournes at Home

I didn't know it then, but that year was his last. Someone a little more sensitive might have read the signs, especially when he said he had lived long enough, when he boasted that he was "imperishable"[2] but his time had come, speaking in a tone of burning rage that I later understood had animated his life and work. That weekend, though, I was shocked to hear a man say he wished it all to end. On those two days in February 1992, he told me some of his stories, explained some of his ideas, and gave me an account of the road he had followed since arriving, a young priest, at the port of Saigon forty-six years earlier.

He greeted me outside the small house he shared with two large dogs, a country bus ride into the hills above the French town of Nîmes. Before leaving Aix-en-Provence, where I was reading colonial archives, I had called from a phone box. Apologizing, I said something had come up, and I'd arrive a week later than planned. I also asked if he'd like me to bring wine. I'd been worrying about the wine for quite a while. What gift do you

---

1. Dournes's *Pötao, une théorie du pouvoir chez les Indochinois jörai* (Paris: Flammarion, 1977) is referred to using the acronym "*PUT*" in footnotes and in-text citations.

2. "Je suis le plus increvable."

take to the author of *Forêt femme folie*?[3] (I had read only one of his books, chosen for its title.) Finally I thought it safer to check.

"Polish vodka," he said emphatically. "Bring Polish vodka."

It was lunchtime. A wiry energetic man came out as I walked across the cracked earth up the garden. The barking of excited dogs almost drowned his gruff, warm welcome. His energy found its first target as I pulled the bottle from my bag:

"What's this blade of grass? The real taste is nothing but grain, nothing but grain."

Knowing little of Polish vodka, I had thought the bison grass a rather good idea.

"And only one bottle," he added. "It's hardly going to see us through the weekend. That's a bottle to drink at a sitting, an hour for two people or two hours alone."

I didn't then know that two men could down a bottle over lunch and still feel the thirst, though I was about to find out.

He brought out rice and an earthenware dish.

"Aubergines. I started cooking them two days before you were to come. They improve day by day. You're late, so they're past their best now, but still good. Sit down."

By now I was feeling more than a little clumsy, out of my depth in the company of this man who spoke exactly what he felt, no more, no less. I was sure of one thing. It was going to be an interesting couple of days.

I had come to see Jacques Dournes on the recommendation of a mutual friend, his former secretary. Marguerita Young had told me of his years in Indochina. "If you're interested in Vietnam, this is someone you should see." At that time, I had no particular interest in the highlanders he'd spent his life studying, and I'd spent only a few weeks in the country, mainly in the capital, Hanoi. Dournes must have sensed this, and I'm now sure he knew I had understood little of *Forêt femme folie*.

"Aha!" he said, "that's my favorite, perhaps because I wrote it for fun, for my own amusement."

---

3. *Forêt femme folie, une traversée de l'imaginaire jörai* (Paris: Aubier-Montaigne, 1978).

Then, kindly he asked, "And what about you? What are you planning to do?"

Stumbling with my words in French, I told him about my work in the archives, my MA dissertation on the economic development of France's Indochina colony, and my current search for a PhD topic: something on the economic history of Vietnam, perhaps? I also asked if he'd spent much time reading documents in the archives in Aix.

"I have more here than they have in Aix," he shot back. "That's why I've never been there. I have more."

It took me some years to realize why such a statement might not be unreasonable.

At the time, I was more conscious of my latest *faux pas*. So I spoke little as he talked of Vietnam and the montagnards, with whom he had lived for many years. His words were not about himself, but revealed much about him: The exile he felt since his return to France, conveyed in a small sense of triumph at the Vietnam postal workers' inability to read the letters he exchanged with his friends, written in Jarai. The failed fusion of Catholic religion and Montagnard civilization attempted in his spiritual quest, a battle decisively won by the latter. The value he placed on "anarchy" and "comedy," reflected in his love for Orwell's *Animal Farm*. His identification with matters of culture and deep dislike of economics. His lively contempt for French media and Parisian academia, for all forms of power, scientific or other.

Between diatribes, with their theatrical repetitions and countless expletives, he sometimes hit the stop button on my recorder to censor a politically sensitive story, to silence some overly virulent outburst. I particularly remember him cutting an account of the purge of people associated with the Pétain regime conducted after 1945 by the French authorities in Saigon with the zealous support of the Catholic Church. He told me that, just off the boat from France, he nonetheless expressed his views about contemporary events, agreeing even with political opinions voiced by Ho Chi Minh. Even then, he did not fit in. Did this explain his choice of mission site—Djiring (today's Di Linh, in Lâm Đồng province), an isolated spot in the hills—where he settled within a few weeks of his arrival?[4] Listening to the tapes now, more than fifteen years on, I can piece together the landmarks of his life.

- Born in 1922, in the Pas-de-Calais region of northern France, of a French father and Swiss mother, into a "bourgeois" family.
- Ordained in 1945.
- Arrived in Vietnam in autumn 1946.
- Deported from Vietnam by Bảo Đại in 1954; returned soon thereafter.
- Left Vietnam for the last time in 1970.
- Defended his thèse d'état ("Pötao, les maîtres des états") in 1973, at the Sorbonne.[5]
- Worked in Paris at the CNRS until his retirement in 1987.

In the words he allowed onto the tapes, Dournes's thoughts range over three subjects: twentieth-century Vietnamese history, his ideas about economy and culture, and montagnard civilization. His monologue was punctuated by my awkward questions, the dogs' barking, and his peals of laughter. These gave a tender quality to his tirades: often, he was laughing at himself. He spoke in a rhetorical style, with repetitions, roars, and whispers. The vowels of the French language rumbled out from deep within his chest. It was a performance in itself. "I am a comedian . . . I know exactly what I am doing," he told me.

The tirades were nonetheless founded on deep anger. It wasn't hard to understand why, back in Paris, former colleagues spoke of his "difficult character" or, more tactfully, his particular "point of view." Intolerant of all, he was clearly patient with this young foreign fool only because of the fool's youth and obvious ignorance, and because I was delighted at his *comédie*.

---

4. See Dournes's comments on this choice in the documentary by Catherine Choron-Baix, *L'homme des Jörai, Vidéo-portrait de Jacques Dournes* (CNRS, 2005).

5. Dournes's PhD dissertation, "Pötao, les maîtres des états, étude d'anthropologie politique chez les jörai," was supervised by Georges Condominas.

I slept the night on a low couch in his front room. Before turning in, he showed me the bathroom, where a wooden medicine cabinet was fixed to the wall above the basin. He pointed to its side panel and, to my surprise, asked me to sign my name there. He asked the same of all who stayed the night. There were perhaps ten names on the list, and as I signed I noticed that Marguerita's was two above mine. I remembered her saying she'd last visited him two years before.

A month later, I left for Vietnam. It was over a year before I returned to France. Better informed now, I realized that Dournes would have fascinating answers to my new questions. I spoke to Marguerita, who told me the news of his recent death (1993). I knew then I would have to rely on his books.

Yet the bibliography of my doctoral dissertation (1999) contains no reference to any work by Dournes.[6] The sad truth is that while I had enjoyed his conversation, I understood little of his written work. How to relate to the "mythological sayings" (dits mythologiques) of his *Florilège srê*?[7] What to make of the forest-girl and plant-woman of *Forêt femme folie*? There was no way in: I found both his French and his methodology perfectly impenetrable.

It was around this time that I first opened *Pötao, une théorie du pouvoir chez les Indochinois jörai*. The first chapters went fine, relying as they did on historical methodology. But as I proceeded through the onion rings of the book's concentric structure, I became increasingly puzzled by its author's use of myths and legends. Like his other books, *Pötao, une théorie* was soon returned to the shelf. It came down again a couple of years later—along with his earlier book *Coordonnées*[8]—during the writing of a book on the montagnards.[9] But still I was unable to grasp the book's argument or fathom its methods. I now know why. I hadn't worked at it hard enough.

6. The dissertation was published under the title *Red Hills: Migrants and the State in the Highlands of Vietnam* (Copenhagen: NIAS Press, 2003).

7. *Florilège srê* (Paris: Sudestasie, 1990).

8. *Coordonnées, Structures jörai familiales et sociales* (Paris: Institut d'Ethnologie, 1972).

9. Mathieu Guérin, Andrew Hardy, Nguyễn Văn Chính, and Stan B.-H. Tan, *Des Montagnards*

Champa and the Montagnards

In 2005, I was becoming interested in the historical relationship between the lowland kingdom of Champa and its mountainous hinterland. Having previously failed to understand *Pötao, une théorie*, and because Champa was not the book's main focus, I little imagined how much light it would shed on this question. So it was not until well into my study that I thought of opening it again.

To illustrate the progress of my research, I have left the following pages, written before this third reading of *Pötao, une théorie*, much as they were when I wrote them in 2004. They form a sort of flashback, dating from a time when I was enjoying the work of Henri Maitre but before I understood Dournes.

In the third century, Champa was described by the Chinese governor of Vietnam with a few succinct strokes of the brush: "Its tribes are very numerous; their friendly bands offer each other mutual help; taking advantage of their mountainous region, they do not submit [to China]".[10] This fragment, however difficult to interpret, offers a perspective confirmed by Champa's later history. Composed of multiple groups, its relationship with the mountainous hinterland differed from the Sino-Vietnamese model, which was a centralized civilization anchored firmly in the plains. By contrast, Champa was politically fragmented and the highlands were an integral part of it.

Champa, we now know, was formed not of "natural *provinces* corresponding to the coastal plains."[11] Rather, its successive plains, separated by mountain spurs, were the heartlands of as many "principalities" (*puras*), each with its own ruler, its own citadel, its own political structure, forming "a sort of federation."[12] It was composed of a multitude of ethnic groups, including the Cham as we understand them today, speakers of Austronesian languages, other people speaking

---

aux Minorités ethniques. Quelle intégration nationale pour les habitants des hautes terres du Vietnam et du Cambodge ? (Paris-Bangkok: L'Harmattan-IRASEC, 2003).

10. Pelliot, "Le Fou-Nan," 255. This "Champa" was of course Lin Yi.
11. Coedès, *Les états hindouisés*, 87 (my emphasis).
12. Po Dharma, *Le Panduranga*, 56.

Austro-Asiatic languages, some living in the plains, and some in the highlands.[13]

Some of the highlanders were indigenous to the hills. Others—the ancestors of today's Jarai people, for example—migrated there at various stages, perhaps shunning newer groups arriving on the plains or avoiding the influence of Indian and Islamic culture. A non-unitary conception of Champa sheds light on the historical relationship of its lowland populations (whose culture was influenced by India) and the highlanders (among whom such influence was minimal). This conception helps move us towards the conclusion that Champa was not confined to the plains, that it embraced parts of the plateaus as well. There was an entity we can call Upper Champa—*le haut Champa*—a term first coined by Jacques Dournes.[14] But what do we mean when we talk of Upper Champa?

Ruins of ancient temples, unearthed in 1984 in Cát Tiên district (Lâm Đồng province), yield a little potentially relevant evidence. In the Đa Đơn river valley, an affluent of the Đồng Nai River and a natural communications corridor between Vietnam and Cambodia, was built the sacred center of a small "principality." The vestiges show artistic influence from eighth-century Champa and Cambodia and religious influence from Hinduism (linga-*yoni* representations, Siva worship).[15] Who built the temples? No historical documents prove that the ancestors of the Mạ people, who inhabited this region of low hills, forests, and marshland, did so. The Mạ today have no memory of them. But for Maitre this was the "Mạ principality"[16] and until recently, the Mạ fiercely defended a sacred territory here, of which they knew nothing but that it was a forbidden, holy place. We have little proof for the idea, but it seems possible that in the past the ancestors of the area's montagnards lived in a much larger area than they do today, an area that may have reached down to the coastal plain between Champa and Cambodia.[17]

---

13. See Gay, "Vue nouvelle," 49–58.

14. Dournes, "Recherches," 143–62.

15. See Nguyễn Tiến Đông, "Khu di tích Cát Tiên ở Lâm Đồng."

16. Maitre, *Les jungles moï*, 431. See also Bourotte, "Essai d'histoire," 31.

17. This idea was proposed by Maitre in *Les jungles moï*, 461–62.

Nguyễn Tiến Đông's analysis of archaeological and topographical data locates Cát Tiên between the Cham and Khmer territories, on the margins of both.[18] Was its relationship to Champa no more than "a vague and distant submission"?[19] Should it be conceived in terms of an "alliance" and if so, what were the terms? Was Cát Tiên a site of one of the principalities of Champa? If we accept any of these models for our understanding, how did it change over time?

Whatever our answers to these questions, it is difficult to avoid concluding that the principality was in relationship with the other regions of Champa, and that these relations included—at the very least—cultural and commercial exchange. Perhaps it even had a place in Champa's network of "multiple riverine estuary and upriver settlements, each a quasi-state with a local ruler who asserted his independence from neighbouring rulers of similar stature."[20]

By extension, we may ask similar questions of the other inhabitants of Champa's highland interior. For the Mạ people, the lowland Cham "were uncles while they stayed in their part of the world, and enemies if they claimed to organize totally the world of the sons of men."[21] The Ra-glai identified themselves much more closely with the Cham, explaining their union through a folktale (see box 1). As for the Jarai, they "lived for centuries in a relationship with the Cham so close that one might wonder which was one and which was the other; the monuments fix the points of reference, oral tradition weaves and covers the people and the centuries, and the Jarai still speak an 'old Cham.'"[22] Vickery suggests that the languages of the Jarai and other Austronesian people were dialects of ancient Cham, later detached from the "mother tongue"; among the Austro-Asiatic groups, meanwhile, "borrowings made from Cham bear witness to fairly close contacts between the two linguistic zones, but also to a degree of Cham presence which differed between regions."[23] If the results of this research can guide our reflection, we may conclude

---

18. Nguyễn Tiến Đông, "Di tích Cát Tiên với Xứ Mạ," 26.

19. Boulbet, *Pays des Maa'*, 72.

20. Guy, "Artistic Exchange," 128.

21. Boulbet, *Pays des Maa'*, 67.

22. Dournes, "Recherches," 155.

23. Vickery, "Histoire du Champa," 24.

that hierarchical relations linked the lowland Cham with the different montagnard groups of the hills.

BOX 1. CHAMPA AND THE RA-GLAI PEOPLE[24]

Jacques Dournes records this folktale of the Ra-glai people. The complex relationship between the Cham and the Ra-glai is described in an allegory of illicit love between a young woman and her parents' servant.

"Choi Koho, go, gather wood with Nai Tolui." Choi Koho is a montagnard, like us. Nai Tolui is a daughter of the Cham country. Choi, the montagnard, and Nai, the Cham, are in love. Choi works as a servant for Nai's parents.

They finish their work and stop at the foot of a tamarind tree, where they notice ripe fruit. Choi bids Nai, "Climb the tree, gather the tamarinds."

The supple Nai climbs, and she settles in a fork, looking at Choi.

"Oh, Nai. How beautiful you are. How can I not desire you when I see you so!"

"Let it be as you wish! Let's live together from now on."

But Nai's parents are not at all of the same opinion. Choi Koho returns to their house.

"What have you done with the axe?" they ask him.

"I forgot it at the foot of the tamarind tree."

"What were you doing at the foot of the tamarind tree?"

"I was looking at Nai Tolui . . ."

"You, Choi, you are only our servant. It will be scandalous if you marry our daughter of Cham blood. It's not done. Find yourself a true montagnard, like yourself, and marry her."

"It is I who desires Choi," replies the girl. "I don't want to be apart from him."

"May you both be cursed! As your punishment, Choi, you will be our slave for life. And you, Nai Tolui, you will die."

The family's old uncle pities the youngsters and wishes to let them live together. He hides them in the forest and tells them to grow corn. "Live in happiness and health, niece and nephew!" On

---

24. Dournes, *En suivant la piste*, 178–79.

the way back he kills a dog, taking the blood to the irascible father so he'll believe the ordered execution has taken place. The forest monkeys help Choi Koho and Nai Tolui clear and plant the land. In a short time, they have a magnificent harvest. They can build a fine house. The uncle comes to see them and he is received with gratitude. A pig is killed in his honor.

Choi and Nai acquire buffalos and horses. These beasts, washing in the river, trouble the waters. Nai thinks of her mother downstream, who won't have good water for drinking. She tells her dog to take her mother a gourd of clean water, attaching it to its collar. The mother, surprised, receives the dog and follows it back to Nai. There, mother and daughter are reconciled. Nai's mother works with her daughter, who is now a person of substance.

The main difference between the inhabitants of the two regions was the influence of Indian culture. Yet, in later centuries, Indianized Cham left monumental proof of their presence on the plateaus: giant brick temples built in the form of towers. The tower of Yang Prong, which still stands near Bản Đôn (Dak Lak), the Kon Klor towers (Kon Tum), and the Yang Mum and Drang Lai towers (Gia Lai), all date from the fourteenth to fifteenth centuries.[25] The settlements around these towers were linked by communications networks, as Maitre found during his investigations of the Cham architectural remains in the highlands.

The vestiges of their occupation still exist and the ruins they left in the interior attest, in these parts, to the extent of their kingdom.

The most interesting discovery is, without any doubt, that of the vestiges of a Cham road, dug into the hillsides, and which must have started at Kon Tum and ended at Quảng Nam, placing the hinterland and the northern provinces of Champa in direct communication. These vestiges are above all visible in the region of Kon Kebau and K. Setiu (Sedang region of the D. Kam valley). Settlements of Cham emigrés were located along this road; the montagnards still know

---

25. Dournes, "Recherches," 146; see pp. 144–55 for descriptions of Champa vestiges in Gia Lai and Kon Tum. The Yang Prong tower is pictured in Nguyễn Văn Kự, Ngô Văn Doanh, and Andrew Hardy, *Peregrinations*, 183. See also Parmentier, *Inventaire descriptif*, 2:17; Hickey, *Sons of the Mountains*, 91–107. Briefer mentions are made in Maitre, *Les jungles moï*, 441, n. 2; Salemink, *Ethnography*, 35.

of the vestiges of four of these settlements. This probably strategic artery had to be abandoned after the fall of Central Vietnam, when the Vietnamese armies occupied Thừa Thiên and Quảng Nam. Finally, a very recent discovery may allow us to fix roughly the area of expansion of Cham occupation; at the beginning of 1911, the ruins of a city said to be Cham were found near the district center of Vœûne-Sai, on the Sesan, although these have not yet been studied.[26]

Yang Mum tower was dismantled by French soldiers around 1930.[27] Even after this event, the local Jarai continued to identify the site with their deities, H'Bia Pe and her brother Pro' Thai, protagonists in a local legend of incestuous love. These are not deities in the Hindu pantheon, but Dournes strongly asserts their significance for our understanding of Jarai-Cham relations: "to follow the trace of H'Bia Pe and her brother is to recognize Jarai implantation here, and to link it to the Cham presence—vestiges in stone and in popular memory."[28] I have no doubt that he was right to identify such links, but more research must be done before we can demonstrate this reading of the Jarai-Champa relationship: that the two were very closely linked. In the meantime, my hypothesis about Yang Mun is that the Jarai later enriched their own animist religious beliefs with worship at the ruins of a temple dedicated to Siva.

The towers were important religious buildings. Their construction implied—at the very least—the existence of large communities in several parts of the highlands: communities that grew food, paid taxes, and supplied labor; communities that could organize masons and sculptors, brickmakers and bricklayers; communities that venerated the Hindu deities. Inscriptions on stone indicate that the temple at Yang Prong was founded with an allocation of fields, slaves, and elephants.[29] As Maitre understood after his 1910 investigation of ruins around the Yang Prong tower, "the temple must have been part of a city, which today

26. Maitre, Les jungles moï, 442–43.

27. Dournes, "Recherches," 151.

28. Ibid., 150–56.

29. Gay, "Vue nouvelle," 52.

has disappeared; a memory of it remains among the Jarai, neighbors to the east."[30]

The inhabitants of this settlement—were they refugees from northern Champa, fleeing territories ceded to the Vietnamese? Were they arriving to establish a base for resistance in the hills? If so, what was the newcomers' relationship with the indigenous inhabitants? Did highlanders worship at the temples? How did they share access to resources?

Finally, were such settlements hubs for Champa rule in this part of the highlands? Did their inhabitants pay taxes and provide services to the plains? Were they sacred sites, situated upstream from the center of Champa civilization, destinations for periodic pilgrimage by the Siva-worshiping faithful? Or were they commercial outposts, stages along the trade routes, places where forest products were dispatched to the ports of the plains? Did they fulfill several of these roles?

The questions come more easily than the answers. It is undoubtedly true that, for ancient Champa, "the mountains perform a double task, both providing a protective shield against aggression from the west and a source of the abundant forest products—most significantly eaglewood—for which Champa was famed from the beginning of its recorded history. The mountains were also crossed by trade routes, along which goods demanded by the long-distance sea traders could be supplied."[31] However we interpret the vestiges, it is difficult to avoid the conclusion that parts of the plateaus formed an important element in the network that was Champa (see box 2).

BOX 2. CHAMPA AND THE MONTAGNARDS[32]

Dournes's first books suggest that the highlands were administratively incorporated into Champa. He later abandoned this view. This text (1950) summarizes his early position.

Having left their islands, the montagnards settled on the continent of today's Indochina, beside the sea, the first land encountered. Their legends suggest that, at that time, they did

---

30. Maitre, *Les jungles moï*, 200.
31. Guy, "Artistic Exchange," 128.
32. Dam Bo (Jacques Dournes), "Numéro spécial consacré," 22–24.

not come into contact with other populations: the place was empty. They were not, however, the first people there. Before them, unknown people had left small spades and flint axes, still discovered from time to time. The montagnards have no idea about this first passage of primitive peoples and attributed a divine origin to these tools that greatly surprised them.

Then the montagnard odyssey notes the Cham on the coast and speaks of them abundantly. But it mentions nothing of their origins. How and from where did they come? Was there fighting with the montagnards? The tradition says nothing, as though this period has been forgotten. We first see the newcomers living on the coast of Vietnam, then learn only of their relations with the Cham, with whom they share the coast and of whom they recognize themselves as vassals, though it is said, "We and the Cham, we are brothers from the same mother." We know from history that this took place in the second century of our era, the first invasion of Indonesians, Hinduized shortly afterwards, leading to the foundation of Champa in Quảng Nam in the year 192.

Then came the fine period of the organization of the montagnards by the Cham, who established administrative divisions led by chiefs they designated. Before, it was complete anarchy; no words even existed in the dialects to express the hierarchy of chiefs, to denote regions in a country. The current words used by montagnards to say "province, province head, canton head" (*lögar, pô lögar, pô prong*) are borrowed from the Cham. The Cham taught the montagnards to grow rice in fields (proven too by Cham influence in this vocabulary). They colonized them, bringing real progress to their frozen, primitive civilization. Inevitably, they required a tax payment from each village, delivered in kind (pigs, blankets, animal hides . . .). Even under the domination of the Vietnamese later on, the montagnards continued to pay their tax to the Cham, who transmitted it in turn to their new suzerain. Moreover, the Cham recruited montagnards as auxiliaries in their army; it was they who carried the arrows shot by the Cham. . . .

During this prosperous period, the montagnard population grew considerably, more so, it seems, than that of the Cham. The montagnards, lacking land (so they explain), left the richer coast to their masters. They advanced, little by little, into the interior, firstly up the eastern slope of the Trường Sơn [Annamitique] Chain, with rich and healthy land; then more deeply, into the forest, organizing the high plateau as far as the region occupied by the Rhadé and the Stieng. It was to this diaspora that they owed the fact they were not Hinduized like the Cham, that they remained more "backward," but also that they survived to the present day, numbering around a million, while the Cham have virtually disappeared.

If we are to fill in the details, we must rely on hypothesis. In his early writings, Dournes presented a historical theory of highland Champa. Drawing from legends, tales, interviews, and linguistic and other oral sources gathered among several montagnard groups, he concluded that, from the earliest days of the Champa kingdom, some montagnards experienced state organization, rendering taxation, labor, and military service (see box 2). Dournes later drew back from these conclusions.[33] Nowhere in his 1970s publications did he make such a case for fully developed state organization: Cham-montagnard relations appear more fluid, less administratively defined in nature. The only exception to this may be observed in his book *Pötao, une théorie,* where he records memories of montagnard liberation from Champa lords in legends surrounding the character Rit (see below).

A second, more geographical theory views the principalities of Champa in terms of terrain and communications. In each principality, river routes linked a coastal port town to a fortified political capital and, further upstream, a religious center with shrines and temples for periodic pilgrimage. The clearest example of this is the civilization situated along the Thu Bồn River in today's Quảng Nam province, including the island of Cù Lao Chàm, a port at Hội An, a political center at Trà Kiệu, and the temple complex at Mỹ Sơn.[34] According to this thinking, the highland towers marked stage posts along routes linking the political and economic centers downstream, both on the

---

33. See Dournes, *En suivant la piste,* 195–97; Dournes, "Recherches"; *PUT,* ch. 4.
34. Trần Kỳ Phương and Vũ Hữu Minh, "Cửa Đại Chiêm," 79.

coast and along the Mekong valley. This interpretation is supported by the map Dournes uses to illustrate *Pötao, une théorie* (*PUT*, 95), where each temple-tower in the hills appears at the head of a river. This theory's focus is on the economic dependence of lowland Champa, particularly in overseas trade and tribute to China, on products of highland provenance.

A third theory regards the highlands as a military rearbase for the lowland Cham—a place of refuge and resistance in case of invasion—where they were helped by the indigenous inhabitants. It dates lowland Champa's permanent presence there to a later period, when wars with the Khmer, a Mongol invasion, and loss of territory to the Vietnamese incited them not only to fight from the hinterland, but also to settle there. The brick towers would be vestiges of this later migration of Indianized Cham.[35] A version of this theory suggests that it was much later, when Champa's disintegration was well advanced, that the montagnards saw the lowland Cham arrive to claim a new role—direct rule in the hills—causing disruption to relations between the ethnic groups. The Mạ people's oral tradition allowed Jean Boulbet to trace the third theory over time, as lowland Champa came under increasing pressure from the Vietnamese (see box 3).

BOX 3. CHAMPA AND THE MẠ PEOPLE[36]

Jean Boulbet's ethno-history of the southern highlands suggests that montagnard responses to Cham arrivals from the plains differed from group to group. Some were content to deal with the newcomers, some retreated, others resisted. This was apparently the case of the Mạ [called Maa'] (located in today's Lâm Đồng province).

- "The Sre people were already administered by vassal notables of the Cham and rendered taxes and services to the people of the plains."

- "Driven to the south of Cape Varella [Mũi Đại Lãnh] by the armies of Huế, the [lowland Cham] needed space and the space of the Maa' is considerable."

---

35. Gay, "Vue nouvelle," 53; Dournes, *En suivant la piste,* 196–97; Dournes, "Recherches," 151, citing Parmentier, *L'art architectural Hindou,* 73.

36. Boulbet, *Pays des Maa',* 67–75.

- "The defeats do not calm the Cham, but on the contrary lead them to seek either a place of refuge or the rump of a kingdom in the interior, where the [Mạ] live."

- For the Mạ, "the Cham are no longer uncles but armed bands defeated on the coast and coming to remake for themselves a fief as extensive as possible."

- "On the plateaus upstream, the great lineages [of the Mạ] divide. Those who consent to remain vassals stay in contact with the Cham; as for the others, they carry their altars to the country downstream, a sparsely inhabited place where great empty spaces separate the villages, which are no more than isles in the enormous forest mass and become centers of resistance."

- "Indirect vassals of the Cham, [some montagnards] serve as intermediaries between the remaining country of the Maa' and the markets of the coast. [But the Mạ] of the northwest . . . organize expeditions into the low country, raiding even the very first Việt who dare to venture into the forests bordering the southern deltas: they recently occupied but rarely leave the fertile, water-logged mud of these deltas that attracted them from the distant north."

The three theories are not mutually exclusive. They also relate to different parts of the highlands, different ethnic groups, different periods of time. And they are far from conclusive. As Maitre discovered, after his 1906 visit to the Yang Prong tower, understanding the montagnards' place in Champa on the basis of such evidence is a treacherous business. After a meeting with the head of a nearby Jarai village, he reported his conversation in terms bordering on despair:

Questioned about the Cham tower of Ya Liao, the head of Tali village declared that it was inhabited by a great spirit—"Yang Prong." He knows the word "Cham" and knows that the warriors of this name had, "excessively long ago," raised this tower when they wanted to make war against the Sadet [Potao]; a small walled city was grouped around the tower, but the Cham, defeated, finished by abandoning the land.[37] Where did they go? Where did they come from? The head had no idea; his fathers had not told him. All he could add was that the Jarai were the first occupants of the soil; they lived for a long time on good terms with the Cham; the arguments later arose over questions of land ownership. One fact is undeniable: the Jarai speak almost pure Cham, but who will ever unravel their history, who will lift the veil which envelopes the origins of the montagnard tribes, the genesis of their different families?[38]

Eschewing despair, we may add a second conclusion to his remarks. Before its coastal centers were lost to the Vietnamese, Champa was a multi-ethnic polity composed of lowland and highland terrains linked by rivers and trails. Within this diverse society, some montagnards maintained a high level of independence; others were more closely integrated into the kingdom. Some enjoyed high status, both religious and political: the best known of these were the Chu-ru and Ra-glai.[39] Others, meanwhile, were "inferiors," perhaps rendering tax in kind and labor to their rulers, more likely exchanging mountain products for salt and other goods.[40] By inferiors here, we should above all think in terms of "exteriors": populations peripheral to the centers of "civilization." We should be careful of making comparisons with today's political concepts: ancient states made fewer and different demands on subjects; there was no single Champa state; between the hills and the plains, contact centered on economic relations. We should be wary, above all, of applying modern terms like "ethnic minority" and "federation" to ancient times.

This equilibrium was upset with the first signs of Champa's decline. Some lowland Cham followed the route taken by the Jarai centuries

37. Dournes finds it inconceivable that the Cham wished to make war on the Potao (Sadet), ascribing this popular memory to a local dispute (*PUT*, 97).

38. Maitre, *Les régions moï*, 220–21.

39. They were nonetheless outsiders, non-Cham, as Dournes notes (*PUT*, 251). They venerated the Cham treasure entrusted to them after Champa's demise, but it was Cham treasure, not theirs.

40. Dournes commented on the Ra-glai legend cited in box 1: "Certainly the Cham considered the montagnards as inferiors: in the legend of Choi Koho and Nai Tolui, the marriage of a Cham chief's daughter with a young montagnard passes for a misalliance; but the Cham were never tyrants. Great prestige made their authority, which was accepted voluntarily" (Dam Bo, "Numéro spécial," 23).

before: they moved to the hills, where long-familiar trading bases provided a sort of refuge. The inhabitants of highlands decided on their attitude to the newcomers: accept, accommodate, or reject the new arrivals. In different cases, different groups and individuals reacted in different ways, and there were limits—as Maitre's remarks about land ownership suggest—to every accommodation. But at the very least, by means of one of the accommodations of that period, an increased population of lowland Indianized Cham in the hills led to the construction, in the fourteenth and fifteenth centuries, of the temple-towers located in the present-day Vietnamese provinces of Dak Lak, Gia Lai, and Kon Tum.

Later, with the kingdom's final collapse, Champa's influence in the hills lapsed. The refugees were confronted with the same stark alternatives. They could discard their lowland culture and stay in the hills. Or they could move on. Many migrated as far as the Mekong, to Cambodia.[41]

By the nineteenth century, however, any montagnard experience of a relationship with Champa was no more than a memory, transmitted by oral tradition, enshrined in religious beliefs and in the Jarai institution of the Potao. A few tangible reminders of the past remained in the form of brick towers. Small stashes of Champa treasure, entrusted by fleeing monarchs, remained in the care of isolated communities.[42] When the French arrived and started documenting highland civilizations, most montagnards remembered nothing of Champa. The brick towers, like the civilization that created them, belonged to a time "excessively long ago."

Only one mention of the book *Pötao, une théorie* was included in the 2004 draft of this text (the others were added later). This was the reference to a map on page 95, which sets the Champa temple-towers in spatial relationship with the territory of the Potao kings of fire, water, and wind. In particular, the map shows the towers' location at the heads of the region's main rivers. Towers could be found at the head of the Sông Ba, flowing

---

41. Mak Phoeun, "La communauté Cam."

42. The Cham treasure held by the Ra-glai in present-day Lâm Đồng is mentioned by Dournes in *En suivant la piste*, 158–60. See also Salemink, *Ethnography*, 36. A bibliography of this question is included in *PUT*, 250, n. 2.

east down to the coast, and at Kon Tum and Yang Prong at the heads of the Sesan and Sepok rivers that drained west to the Mekong. As I looked at the map then, the towers seemed to mark stage posts along a communications route across the hills. And reading it now, the location of the Cham towers and Potao territory near the heads of the rivers were clearly no coincidence. The river valleys formed a major route for travel and trade through the Central Highlands for many centuries even after the decline of Champa.[43]

The Jarai Potao

This was the extent of my understanding when I re-opened *Pötao, une théorie* in 2005. As I read, I learned much about the Champa-montagnard relationship, embedded in various mentions scattered through the book. But this interest in Champa gradually gave way to a curiosity about the Potao themselves. The key lay in the book's middle section, particularly chapters 6 and 7. Here, Dournes presents analysis of Jarai tales and myths about the Potao. It was precisely at this point in the book that I had stumbled in the past, stymied by the methodology. Now I learned about the man Rit, about the woman H'Bia, the different cultural manifestations of the Potao, and the meanings of the myths. Immediately after putting the book down, I wrote a summary of my understandings, linking it to the "flashback" text presented above.[44]

> One of the most important montagnard institutions, founded "excessively long ago" but surviving to the time of Dournes, was that of the Potao: the Jarai "kings" of fire, water, and wind.
>
> In the centuries after the decline of Champa, the Khmer monarch saw these Potao in both religious and secular terms, as his spiritual superiors but also as the leaders of a vassal people responsible, in their strategic position along east-west communications, for "keeping the

---

43. Dournes confirms this (*PUT*, 30), quoting Cupet's notes: "in the past, the ox-carts went as far as where the Sadets [Potao] live," then adding: "an interesting piece of information, the trail . . . effectively constituted the route for travel in the direction of Sambok" on the Mekong.

44. Here too, I have made minimal modifications to this "flashback" text originally written in 2005.

trails." Emissaries were regularly dispatched. Gifts were exchanged at a site beside the Mekong (*PUT*, 104–9, 137–41).

Vietnam's kings, meanwhile, integrated the "kings of fire and water" into their model of rule, based on the Chinese tributary system. The Potao were given the rank of prince and diplomatically engaged through tributary gifts exchanged at the court of Huế. Their status was inflated to meet the need for dependent kingdoms within an imperial "Sino-Vietnamese dream-fabric."[45] Thus was suzerainty established over kingdoms that did not exist (see *PUT*, 9, 84).

In no way did these relations imply, to the montagnards, integration into lowland feudal systems. And yet, most significantly, they entered freely into these relations: their emissaries bore tribute to distant courts, dressing appropriately before foreign kings. Their participation suggests that they too were weaving a dream-fabric. Interpreting lowland marks of respect into their networks of alliances, incorporating tributary relations into their imagination, they approved that others—in their foreign way—should esteem the Potao as they did.

How were the Potao esteemed among the Jarai? If they were not kings, were they no more than "powerful shamans with a religious and ritual status that was recognized by surrounding populations"?[46] Yet in these societies where the political and the spiritual were indissoluble, the Potao had more than ritual importance. The people lived in awe of their Potao's relationship with the gods and the catastrophes that might follow transgression. The Potao lived frugally; his wealth was spiritual; his prestige required none of the luxury paraphernalia associated with conventional kingship. We may agree that he was the guarantor of a politico-religious order. But when the Potao stood for the sacrifice, sat for the ritual chant, made his tour of the villages, what order did he guarantee?

Dournes subtitled his book on the Potao "A Theory of Power." The choice of subtitle is significant. How did montagnards think about power? How did outsiders relate to their political systems? For the Jarai at least, Dournes's book is the nearest we get to an answer.

The book presents a survey of Western and Southeast Asian writing on the Potao, followed by analysis of myths and legends in the

---

45. Woodside, *Vietnam and the Chinese Model,* 238.
46. Salemink, *Ethnography,* 36.

montagnard oral tradition. Many legends turn around the relationship between four characters: the *kotang* (a strongman possessing a sacred sword), the *potao* (a lord), H'Bia (a woman), and "the unexpected figure of Rit, the poor little orphan, who is the intended victim of the potao[-lord]."[47] These themes have been summarized as follows:

> Through the miraculous intervention of "the inhabitants of the forest," Rit has come to acquire not only some possessions but also the beautiful H'Bia, the embodiment of Jarai womanhood and Jarai culture. The tyrannical local potao covets all that Rit has, but when he attempts to seize his belongings he is thwarted by the wily Rit, who, in the end, wins over the tyrant. But unlike the powerful kotang, he does not seize the authority of the local lord. The possession of power is not his goal; he prefers to remain the simple unencumbered man.[48]

Dournes bases his interpretation on a set of oppositions and conflations relating to these characters. A first opposition is made between the Potao as the living master of the sacred rites, and the *potao* of the mythical past, imagined lords and tyrants. The distinction between the present and the past is then conflated, and we learn that the Potao is both: "when the Jarai speaks of the sacred Potao, he cannot avoid thinking of the *potao* of myth" (*PUT*, 186).

A second opposition distinguishes the *potao*-lord (signifying a particular political institution, but also political institutions in general) from the man Rit (representing the people). Rit is conceived as the anti-*potao*, the Jarai people's opposition to political institutions (*PUT*, 153). The story ends with Rit's victory over the institutions and—after he refuses to seize them for himself—with their abolition: "The Potao collapses. The Master becomes a slave . . . but cannot even find a master" (*PUT*, 180).

The religious leader of real life (Potao) thus bore the name of the abolished institution of myth (*potao*), precisely because he embodied the abolition of all political institutions. In this conflation, he became Rit, "the incarnation of Jarai independence" (*PUT*, plate 4, opposite p. 144). He was neither a political nor religious leader: he was both,

---

47. Hickey, *Sons of the Mountains*, 134.
48. Ibid.

and the antithesis of both. As an institution, his power among the Jarai resided in his elimination of institutionalized power (see box 4).

BOX 4. THE TALE OF RIT, H'BIA, AND THE POTAO[49]

Rit goes hunting with his dog. There was no game that day, but he brought home a section of bamboo. During one of Rit's absences, out of the bamboo comes a beautiful young girl, named Arondine (H'Bia Jorao, evocative of the swallow and the water nymph), who weaves for him and prepares a meal. Rit manages to surprise her. They live happily together . . . until the day when the potao-lord learns through his intelligence service that a very beautiful woman lives with Rit. He wants that woman. He forces Rit into trials of strength, expecting his death. Thanks to a talisman stone, Rit obtains magic weapons from a local lord. Rit succeeds in the trials of strength. Finally, the lord insists that Rit go to bring him the daughters of Thunder and Lightening; he could then retrieve his Arondine. Thunder and Lightening can do nothing against Rit. They give him their daughters, then go and fight the lord. All these potao disappear in a cataclysm. (*PUT*, 180–81)

In the legends, this struggle was presented in the mythical past, as a set of historical events. Rit thus appeared as a Jarai hero of the past, the cataclysm's sole survivor. The potao-lord and other figures of power like the lords named Thunder and Lightning were assimilated to the Cham or other outsiders (*PUT*, 160, 187). Yet the past tense acted as a veil to the legend's availability "as a possibility open in all times" (*PUT*, 190). Thus the mythical past is also present; hence Dournes's use of the present tense in his translations, as in box 4. On the basis of this conflation of time, Dournes formulated his theory of the sacred Potao as the permanent political institution the Jarai created for themselves. This theory is summarized in the citations below.

---

49. Dournes published many such tales in *Pötao, une théorie,* as well as in *Akhan, Forêt femme folie,* and other volumes.

- Guardians of tradition, guarantors of non-change, the Potao of today, have rendered the authority of a government useless (an outmoded stage). They are the façade of conformity behind which the people have the leisure of projecting the transgression of the institution that they have given themselves. But . . . it is when the Jarai people treat their [sacred] Potao as Potao[-lords] that they transgress—which leads to the conclusion that their true institution is to have no institution. This is only an apparent contradiction, as the myths offer a solution in the form of [Rit,] the anti-potao as a type of ante-potao: $P + P^{-1} = 0$. This is not nothingness, but equilibrium. (*PUT*, 191)

- That which the woman is to the family—permanent base, continuity, trace of the past, prolonged tradition, force of resistance to all attack from outside—constitutes the "warp" of the sociopolitical structure; it is the inside, and also the underside for the outsider. On his side, the man—husband and son, fire and air—being the changing element and the factor of relation between the clans (matrimonial alliances) by his to-ing and fro-ing, represents—as "weft"—Jarai politics, establishing alliances with neighbors, attempting compromises with their civilization. In all this, he remains on the surface, of which the "underside" is a remarkable independence, under the cover of the Potao: heads of state for those who call them Samdach or Vua [in Khmer and Vietnamese], purely religious heads for those who deride their "majesty," guarantee of the smooth running of the system for the Jarai. (*PUT*, 323)

- Under the appearance of institutions and behind fixations with the Potao (the politico-religious) and with H'Bia (the familial) as barriers keeping anarchy from degenerating into disorder, the final sociopolitical reality is perhaps this elusive and ungovernable freedom, the subtle game of one who seems to conform while doing what he wishes, laughing at Power, at Order, and at himself—as revealed in the gestures of the festivals and the situations of the myths. The final "cover" removed, there remains none but Rit, naked and alone, searching for that which the Powerful want to steal from him: his dream, his life, H'Bia. (*PUT*, 327)

Two further conclusions emerge from Dournes's analysis. The first concerns the origins of the Potao institution. May we speculate that this institution was created through a process of relation with the power-holders of lowland Champa (in Cham, the word *potao* means lord)?

Dournes does not venture so far—not directly at least. According to this hypothesis the Jarai found it convenient to invent a supra-village political entity, equipping themselves thus with an interlocutor for the *potao* lords of the plains.

Secondly, reading this one wonders how many Jarai could see themselves in such complex and contradictory formulae, and how well Western theory is suited to the search for understanding of montagnard societies. But among the many merits of Dournes's work is a view of what he calls the "underside": an endogenous explanation for the difficulties encountered by outside states in their relations with montagnards.

Under the Nguyễn dynasty, we have seen, these consisted of "dream-fabric." As distant neighbors, both sides could weave the realities of the relationship into the fabric of their own imagination. On these terms, the montagnards could welcome the overtures of outsiders.

In the twentieth century, imagination was lost, dream-fabrics increasingly impossible. Forest trails became motorable roads, travel increased in facility and frequency, states replaced tribute with tax. Montagnards no longer needed to ply the salt trails: Vietnamese and Chinese shops opened in the hills. With these flows came attempts to penetrate Jarai institutions, bring administration to their villages, remold their rituals, co-opt their Potao as collaborators of the state. Dournes's theory helps explain the accommodations through which montagnards accepted foreign incursions into their world. It also sheds light on the moments when such accommodations failed to bear fruit.

Looking back on these notes today (2009), Dournes's work appears remarkable precisely because it lives up to the promise of its title, offering a theory of montagnard power. The book is a work of structural anthropology, the French strand of which was led by Claude Lévi-Strauss, and applied "hard science" methodologies to the study of human societies. Structural anthropology posited the existence of fundamental structures of human thought. These, moreover, were often identified in binary terms—as sets of opposites/oppositions—which feature with great regularity in Dournes's work. Nowadays structural anthropology is commonly critiqued for its ahistorical approach, in which the existence of fixed structures denies the possibility of change over time.

My ignorance of structural anthropology had defeated my early attempts to read *Pötao, une théorie*. It seemed now, however, that Dournes's handling of it had contributed a great deal to our knowledge. Even the ahistorical perspective might be useful in the identification of continuities over time. Readers of *Pötao, une théorie* should however be aware of the use of binaries—they appear often, both in Dournes's book and my discussion of it here—and of the need to balance the existence of continuities with the realities of historical change.

In early 2009, two conversations with the writer Nguyên Ngọc helped improve my understanding of the book. Our first exchange may be summarized as follows.

Central to the question was the division between the inside and the outside, between the male and female in the matrilineal system. The female holds power, but in public she stays in the background, delegating communication with outside to a male relative.[50] People make the distinction between male thunder and female lightning: thunder makes a lot of noise, but no one has ever been struck down by it. The Potao, however, embodies both male and female principles. On the inside, he does not play the role of king, but his prestige is real (he is lightning, not thunder). With regard to outsiders, however, he is not a king but happy to appear as one (he is thunder but happy to appear as lightning). He lets others imagine him as they wish, enters into diplomatic relations, and sends out ambassadors.

In our second conversation, Nguyên Ngọc explained his ideas more fully. During a seminar presentation, he set the Potao in the context of the Jarai village political system, where two leaders divide political responsibilities for exterior and interior affairs. A secular leader (*khoa buon*) meets outsiders, appearing to be the village head, while its real power holder—a spiritual leader (*khoa yang*)—remains hidden. The Potao combined both functions: for the Jarai, he was both *khoa buon* and *khoa yang*, both exterior and interior, secular and spiritual, male and female, Rit and H'Bia.

50. See Dournes, *Forêt femme folie*, ch. 2, especially p. 27: "he is relation, with the other, with elsewhere. Woman is departure and completion, end."

Just after the seminar, we discussed the question with a young journalist. We agreed that understanding the Potao's relations with outsiders was the easier task. It was harder to grasp how his power worked at home. Our reply to the journalist's question may be summarized as follows:

> When we think about the Potao, the key word is harmonizing. The Potao harmonized on several different levels, with nature, with the gods, with the people, setting each in relation with the other. If we look at the way his power worked at the level of human society, it was not as a mighty leader (*potao*-lord) but as Rit, the weakest of men. Because he listens to the people, the people listen to him. He doesn't decide, he harmonizes, and that is the source of his prestige and power.

Dournes himself found a more concrete way of expressing this truth, in a discussion of the succession to the king of wind (Potao *angin*), who had died around 1945. The people grumbled about the acting Potao, designated but yet to be anointed. They said it didn't rain enough, the spirit didn't rest on him, he was too distantly related to the Siu clan from which the Potao had to be chosen. Eventually a "group of influential elders" and the Potao's ministers took matters in hand and chose a different man, Chobba, who corresponded to the people's preference. Dournes commented:

> It all happens as though, deep down, the people could alone change the situation, and in the way they chose, while leaving the various authorities the appearance of having managed everything; family affairs are also run according to this model, whereby the woman decides and does everything under cover of the man, who is her spokesman and takes center stage. Once she has children, a Jarai woman could do without a husband—and has no hesitation in saying so—except that a husband saves her being courted by other men. The Jarai people could do without the Potao, if he was not there precisely to save them from falling under the sway of governors, with the difference that the Potao is a little more master than the man in the house, as he is both father and mother. (*PUT*, 256)

The Potao was a political institution in this apparently contradictory sense. At home in Jarai country, he played the woman's role (H'Bia).

With outsiders, he played the man's role, calling himself Potao, a title that evoked the Cham word for lord and master (*potao*).

On both occasions, Nguyên Ngọc and I agreed that as an institution of power, the Potao institution was deeply unfamiliar to us. It also operated on many different levels. Dournes reminds us throughout the first part of his book that none of his predecessors in the study of the Potao had achieved an understanding of it. But then, none of them had given fifteen years of their life to the attempt.

One of Dournes's successors, however, made a study that sheds contemporary light on the functioning of this institution. This was the anthropologist Oscar Salemink, who did fieldwork in Gia Lai province in 1991, during which time he visited the designated replacement for the king of fire (Potao *apui*; *p'tau pui* in Salemink's account).[51] Oi Nhot had died four years earlier.[52] However, his successor, Siu Aluan, could not be named Potao before the ritual ceremonies of consecration had been performed: the Jarai were awaiting authorization for the buffalo sacrifices that these would entail. Siu Aluan's wife, at the same time, was lamenting her fate. When he was named Potao, she knew she would have to divorce him. The Potao had to be of the Siu clan and his wife of the Rmah clan, but she belonged to the Rcom clan.

At the time of Salemink's visit, the ceremony was expected within a few months. At the same time, the authorities had their own plans for the ceremony and the Potao: the rituals would be filmed; the sacred swords, hidden in a nearby hill, would be moved to a temple for safekeeping and exhibition; the Potao's village, Plei P'tau, would be turned into a museum, its longhouses intact, for the benefit of tourists. Salemink commented:

According to the procedure of "selective preservation," these plans implied that the beliefs and practices surrounding the *p'tau pui* had been promoted on the scale of customs to be preserved rather than

---

51. This and the following paragraphs are based on Salemink's account in *Ethnography*, 282–87.

52. In Vietnamese, Oi Nhot's name is rendered as Siu Nhŏt. The name Oi in Jarai translates as "ông" in Vietnamese and is used for the Potao (Oi Nhŏt) and his village (*plơi* Oi, or Plei P'tau in Salemink's account). Siu Nhŏt's successor, Siu Aluân, is known in Vietnamese as Siu Luynh (Nguyễn Thị Kim Vân, "Hiện tượng Lịch sử," 20, 28).

eradicated. The *p'tau pui* would be officially branded a valuable part of traditional Jarai custom, while Jarai society moved forward on the shiny path toward socialism, or—nowadays—the market. Detached from the developments taking place around them, the inhabitants of the village would act out a living past, with their village standing as a monument of this very past, conforming to the official version of Jarai traditional life.[53]

He then asked, "How does Siu Aluan feel about the plans concerning himself and his village?"

The answer is revealing. Salemink found that Siu Aluan greatly valued his contacts with the authorities. Far from resenting the "deal" imposed as a condition for the ceremony's approval, he welcomed the plans, expecting to receive a government medal as his predecessor had received from the French, the Americans, and the Republic of Vietnam. At first, Salemink was puzzled by this attitude: "His consent to become a museum character, on display for a varied audience, may at first sight seem a travesty of Jarai culture, a commodification of Jarai cultural concepts for the benefit of Vietnamese and foreign consumers." But the anthropologist understood that "through his subordination to Vietnamese cultural politics, his religious status is implicitly recognized," sensing that in the present as in the past the existence of the Potao "shored up claims to territorial, political and cultural autonomy for the Highlanders."

This fieldwork was conducted a few months before I visited Dournes, in the early 1990s. Reading Salemink's account, I wondered what Dournes would have said. Today I can almost hear him roar at both Salemink and me, with our academic seriousness: "Imbeciles! It's just comedy!" The nineteenth-century Potao had been comfortable sending envoys to Huế, playing along with the Vietnamese fantasy that they were real kings. They even switched the names and geographical locations of the kings of fire and water, causing further confusion at the Vietnamese court.[54] And so now, with the same equanimity, they accepted the terms of this twentieth-

---

53. Salemink, *Ethnography*, 285.
54. In Huế, the fiction was discovered in 1841 and blamed on an interpreter (*PUT*, 119). Dournes, however, saw this as more than a mistake, speculating that it was a deliberate act of concealment by the Jarai (*PUT*, 277).

century game. All this comedy was for the benefit of foreigners; it was of no real significance. Or rather, its significance was to humor outside powers, ensuring the perpetuation of the truly important things at home: that the rituals be performed, that the Potao tour the villages, that the relation between people, nature, and the gods remain in harmony, unharmed, that this extraordinary institution continue to guarantee the prosperity and independence of the Jarai.

Given that by the 1990s the Potao no longer toured the villages, it is more likely that Dournes would have reacted as he did to a stunt of the Vietnam War period, when the Saigon authorities staged an airdrop at a landing strip near Plei Ku. A crate landed on the airstrip. Then from an identical crate hidden just behind the one that had just fallen from the sky emerged the king of fire. "Unpardonable for the Jarai," Dournes growled (*PUT*, 202).[55] Did these words convey his recognition of the limits, the decline even, of the Potao's power? Or, when he penned them, had he momentarily lost his sense of humor?

One final question: why was the ceremony not approved? Was the decision based upon a reticence "about competing political claims in a strategic region"?[56] Or perhaps, as Salemink speculates, the matter got bogged down in cautious bureaucracy and no decision was ever made. In any case, the ceremony was not held and Siu Aluan never had to divorce his wife. He died in 1999. Five years later it was reported that "the Potao Apui's paraphernalia are held at Ơi village by Siu [Aluan's] assistant Rơlan Hieo."[57]

The Jarai Constitution

In his account of the Potao, Salemink does not analyze the institution itself. He refers us instead to Dournes's book.[58] For the reader of Salemink who has yet to tackle Dournes, the laments of Siu Aluan's wife are comprehensible only as the result of an inhumane system of kinship rules.

---

55. But on the same page, Dournes contradicts himself, commenting on a similar incident that "foreigners do not know, their comedy is thus of no importance."

56. Salemink, *Ethnography*, 286.

57. Nguyễn Thị Kim Vân, "Hiện tượng Lịch sử," 28.

58. Salemink, *Ethnography*, 259, n. 2.

Dournes's analysis not only allows us to make sense of Siu Aluan's wife's situation. It also sheds light on the Jarai in their historical relationship with Champa.

In part B of chapter 10 (entitled "Permanence"), Dournes presents the cultural specificities that ensured the institution's continuity. These specificities include the relationship between the three Potao, each with his own territory, his own sacred treasure, his own particular symbolism and gendered attributes, his own ministering officials. Thus we see Dournes analyzing the Potao in the form of a table (*PUT*, 280; see table 1 below), listing their respective attributes.

Table 1. Attributes of the Potao

Potao *ia* [King of Water]	Potao *apui* [King of Fire]	Potao *angin* [King of Wind]
ami' (mother)	*ama* (father)	*ana'* (son)
ronang (calm)	*kotang* (strong)	*kotang hloh* (stronger)
root (cold)	*holor* (hot)	neither hot nor cold
west	east	more east

The oppositions are clear: Potao *apui* is force of fire, Potao *ia* is calm of water; Potao *apui* is male, Potao *ia* is female; Potao *apui* guards the sabre, Potao *ia* keeps the sheath. Complementarity is also maintained, not only in the straightforward correspondence between sword and sheath (the sexual connotation is not lost), but also in reversed, apparently self-contradictory forms. For example, Potao *apui* (sword) is hidden (but he is male), Potao *ia* (sheath) is visible (but he is female).

Why this complex system of opposition and complement? Dournes tells us that complementarity denies the possibility of hierarchy: "To ask which of the Potao *apui* or Potao *ia* is the greatest or the more important comes down to asking which is the greatest, man or woman—which has no meaning in Jarai society. Man is apparently set before and above, because it is in fact on the woman that all rests, despite the fact that she does not show herself, like the sabre—which constitutes one of the chiasma dear to Jarai style, which crisscrosses symmetries" (*PUT*, 276–77).

Dournes also shows that the two Potao do their best to avoid meeting or entering each other's territory. If such an event took place, it was carefully prepared with the dispatch of gifts. The relationship between them is "ambiguous, as between fire and water, as between husband and wife (who do not even touch each other in public)." He then introduces the third Potao, because "it was necessary to imagine a third to arrange matters, by making them more complicated" (*PUT*, 276). For Dournes, as the table shows, the Potao *angin* is the son; among his attributes are wind, war, and great strength.

Potao symbolism draws from the realm of economic activities as well. Here too the attributes are gendered: Potao *apui* is the blacksmith (male), Potao *ia*, the blacksmith's assistant (female); Potao *apui* is the basketmaker (male), Potao *ia*, the weaver (female). As for Potao *angin*, to him devolves the use of these objects: "it is appropriate to the son (who is not productive) and the warrior (who destroys) to be on the side of consumption-destruction" (*PUT*, 279).

The obsession with classifying appears in numerous taboos on what the Potao and his ministers ate and drank, the clothes they wore, their living arrangements, and moral behavior: no joking with women, no participation in the rowdy festivities of the tomb ceremony. It appears too in the socio-familial arrangements determining the choice of the man chosen as Potao: "the clan of the three Potao and their wives is imperiously fixed." Dournes illustrates these in another table (*PUT*, 284; see table 2 below).

Table 2. Potao clan and affinity

Potao *ia*	Potao *apui*	Potao *angin*
Rcom	Siu	Sui
married to a Siu	married to a Rmah	married to a Rmah

The question of clan allowed Dournes to represent schematically the Potao as father, mother, and son, with the clan name passed down the mother's line (*PUT*, 284; see fig. 1 below).

Fig. 1. Lineage chart showing Potao clans and affinity

This "imperiously fixed" rule governing the choice of Potao, moreover, is only one of this type of arrangement. For the Potao, the key clan is Siu, assisted by Rcom and Rmah. Each clan has its own function. Among the other four of the seven Jarai clans, the Kosor nominate the Potao's ministers and the Nei prepare the rituals. Only the Rahlan and the Kopa, "originally from the southeast and southwest of Jarai country, are like strangers to the central Jarai group" (*PUT*, 286). This remark leads Dournes to his final diagram, where concentric circles situate each Jarai, through their clan membership, in a hierarchical relationship to the three Potao at the center. "This is exactly what happens during the ritual, like a game of waves which, through the ministers, links the Potao to the population of each clan" (*PUT*, 286). It also resembles the onion-ring model Dournes chose to structure his book, starting with the remotest outsiders (Europeans), moving through the nearer neighbors (Champa, Cambodia, Vietnam) before finally closing in on neighboring montagnard peoples and the Jarai themselves.

A similar set of concentric circles also linked the population, through the Potao, to the gods. The people could call directly on the lower-level spirits, *yang* (like the Catholic saints?). The Potao's ministers had access to the senior divinities, Po (including the Potao). The Potao in turn invoked the Lord of Heaven, Adei, and the goddess H'Bia (like the Christian Trinity?). In Dournes's analysis, this spiritual dimension comes as an afterthought to his description of the sociological reality (inside) and the politico-diplomatic instrument (outside). Indeed, analysis of spiritual beliefs and practices is all but absent from Dournes's oeuvre. But he acknowledges that all three dimensions worked towards the maintenance of Jarai socioethnic identity.

As though wishing to justify this ultra-complex analysis, Dournes remarked: "The Jarai, who are keen on classifications, make infinite cuts (*découpages*) only then to re-link the pieces (*recoupements*), symbolizing in yet another way the repartition of functions between the Potao" (*PUT*, 278). Salemink illustrates the *découpages-recoupement* process in the story of Siu Aluan's wife. She shed tears as she found herself caught by one of the *découpages* that linked the Potao to the population, giving systemic coherence to the Jarai village communities. A mere cog in the system, she herself did not benefit from the corresponding *recoupement* enjoyed by the community. Quite simply, she was from the wrong clan. And she was not the first to make the sort of sacrifice the system required. In the 1940s succession case mentioned above, Dournes relates how the new Potao *angin*, Chobba, "had to leave his village and his wife, who is from the Kosor clan, to settle at Plöi 'Mang and take a Rmah wife as the custom prescribes" (*PUT*, 256). In the 1990s case, Salemink reported nothing about Siu Aluan's wife's feelings at her misfortune. During the long wait for her husband's accession, was she relieved as approval was delayed? Did the fear of personal tragedy blind her to the community's greater loss? For her, it must have been a time of conflicting emotions.

At this point, these arrangements seemed to amount to more than a mechanism for the maintenance of community identity. They appeared to be a constitution, in the British sense, where nothing is formally written down; there are just known and accepted political arrangements. It then occurred to me that if I had thought of this, then certainly the idea must have crossed Dournes's mind. I checked. Chapter 10, where these arrangements are described, is entitled "The Constitution of the Regime."

Questions Raised by *Pötao, une théorie*: A Cosmology Shared with the Cham?

All these insights—into Rit, Potao, and the Jarai constitution—I gained during my later readings of *Pötao, une théorie*. I also gathered other knowledge, gleaned along the way from the author's habit of slipping key observations almost haphazardly into the text, of firing off asides about issues that were marginal to his main story. This is another of the book's difficulties: the wide range of the author's peripheral vision.

At the same time, I returned to our conversation in 1992. Transcribing the tapes, I felt relieved to be his junior. He had been much kinder to me than he was, even in print, to his predecessors in the field.[59] The tapes contain no information about the Potao. There are a few minutes on the montagnard trading economy and the ancient "salt trails" to the coast. There was also a lively warning against overly economic interpretations of montagnard civilization, of Vietnamese civilization, and indeed of civilization in general:

> Rice is not a value. And cooking rice is not a value. It's a necessity, just like when you poo, no? Every day I eat my rice, everyday I poo, everyday I eat my chilli. These things are mechanical, biological. No one cares. It's natural, it's simple, you don't talk about it, it's of no interest.
>
> When you're free in the evening, at night, or when it's raining too much and you can't go out, you drink! You invent a heap of fine things, the Holy Grail, the Song of Roland, Tristan and Isolde, etc. The economic side to all that? It's anti-economic. It's free. . . . It's pure creation and creation is free by definition.

Listening again, years after our conversation, I took heed of the warning. I had felt that the clearest story of Champa-era upland-lowland relations was to be told through its trading system, simply because the historical and anthropological evidence exists: Champa's commercial system survived for centuries after the kingdom's political demise.[60] Dournes recognized this but contrasted it with the domain, as he put it, of the "anti-economic": "What interests me is culture, oral literature, myths and people, epic tales, all that people tell and that they are able to think. So the economy, pfzz!

---

59. See the early chapters of *Pötao, une théorie*. Captain Cupet ("fairly well informed," 28), Georges Condominas ("meticulous pen," 55), Norman Lewis ("a gift for flair and humor," 47) and others earn praise for a telling detail or instinct, but generally he is merciless. Authors are held to account for their every word and often openly derided.

60. See Hardy, "Eaglewood," 107–26.

Obviously they had an economy.... It's another world."[61] When he spoke in this way, what he meant of course was that he was not interested. Today our discussion would be more heated, especially as I would challenge this posturing about economics, as I would his neglect of Jarai spiritual beliefs. Certainly in 1992, he did not pull his punches: "Economists, I can't stand them, any more than sociologists, any more than ethnologists, because too often they speak of things they don't know." But Dournes the ethnologist speculated too: he hazarded asides and voiced his instincts. At the risk, then, of speaking of things I do not know and meriting his contemptuous "pfzz!" let me venture off the familiar terrain of Champa-montagnard trading relations and raise a further question elicited by my readings of *Pötao, une théorie*.

This question arose from the way Dournes considered the attributes of the respective Potao as of little importance in themselves. The vital thing was the relations between them (*PUT,* 287). Digesting this idea I recalled—in the manner of a deja-vu—a similar set of relations elsewhere, in a study made by the anthropologist Rie Nakamura. Her work on the Cham people described cosmological relations that might bear comparison with the Potao.[62]

During 1995 fieldwork in Ninh Thuan province, Nakamura identified a cosmology consisting of pairs of oppositions and conflations. In her account, the Cham Balamon (following an indigenized form of Hinduism) and the Cham Bani (adhering to an indigenized form of Islam) see their world in terms of two principles. The Balamon are *ahier,* which is the male principle; the Bani are *awar,* female. These binary oppositions may be listed in a Dournes-style table (see table 3).

At the same time, the gap created by these opposites was bridged. In a system of "complementary dualism," each side contained a feature normally associated with the other. Everything is either *ahier* or *awar,* male or female, yet everything must also bear "attributes representing

---

61. This citation and the one in the following paragraph have been excised from the transcript of my conversation with Dournes but appear in the original French in the appendix.

62. Nakamura, "*Awar-Ahier,*" 78–106. These paragraphs summarize Nakamura's chapter; I have referenced only the direct citations.

something from the opposite sex."[63] Thus Balamon priests (*ahier*, male) carry a rectangular bag symbolizing the uterus, and Bani priests (*awar*, female) carry three bags symbolizing the penis and testicles. Thus in *ahier* ceremonies *ahier* Balamon priests pray to *awar* Bani gods and present *awar* offerings. The point is interdependency: the relations between the attributes mold Bani and Balamon into a coherent Cham whole, unified in complementary opposition.

Table 3. *Ahier* and *awar* attributes

Ahier	Awar
male	female
back/behind	front/before
Cham Balamon	Cham Bani
a linga turban, worn by priests	a *khan djram* woman's turban, worn by priests
the upper body	the lower body
no. 3	no. 6 (*the sum forms the most complete number, 9*)
Sunday/Monday/Tuesday	Thursday/Friday/Saturday (*Wednesday is neutral*)
dawn to noon	noon to sunset

Like Dournes, Nakamura applies a caveat to Cham cosmology: the relations between the attributes are more important than the attributes themselves. In one of her examples, succession to the Bani priesthood's highest office (*ong guru*) was subject to strict rules relating to the aspirant's wife. At the time of Nakamura's visit to a Bani village, the office of *ong guru* had long been vacant, and the villagers were unable to organize several important rituals as a result. But unlike in the Jarai case, the wait was not caused by delayed authorization. Nakamura reports: "The reason for this situation was both simple and, to me, unexpected. The wife of the candidate for the position of Ong Guru was very sick, lying in hospital." She explained that women and unmarried men may not enter

---

63. Nakamura, "*Awar-Ahier*," 90.

the priesthood, and "Bani priests can be promoted only if their wives are healthy and have good moral conduct."[64]

The aspiring *ong guru* suffered a double distress. His wife was sick, and her illness was delaying his promotion and the community's rituals. According to complementary dualism—the inclusion of a female element within the male principle (and vice versa)—she was an irreplaceable part of the relation on which his religious purity was based. Without her, it was better the ceremonies not be held.

Later, focusing on the Bani, Nakamura noted a shift in *awar-ahier* relations: the genders were reversed. Then in a further shift, the gender attributes disappear when a third element (*akafir*) is introduced. The attributes then connote the individual's relative distance from the deity, Po Alwah. "Bani priests (*Awar*) enjoy the greatest proximity to *Po Alwah*, the Bani lay people (*Ahier*) are the next closest, and the Cham Balamon (*Akafir*) exist at the greatest distance."[65] Non-Cham people do not figure in the model. They are simply non-Cham.

She drew the following conclusion about the significance of her findings:

> [The fluidity of these terms] illustrates the interdependency of the two religions of the Cham people living in the south central region. At a glance, *Cham Balamon and Bani seem like two completely different religions, of Hindu and Islamic origin, but they are in fact two different outcomes of acculturation grown in the same ground.* Cham Balamon religious attributes make sense only when in opposition to Bani religious attributes, and vice-versa. For the Cham people of South Central Vietnam, this binary principle is the dynamic that constructs their world.[66]

Sharing a belief system, a sense of belonging to the old kingdom of Champa and a common ancestry, both Bani and Cham Balamon assert a common ethnicity to outsiders.[67]

---

64. Ibid., 94.
65. Ibid., 96.
66. Ibid., 97.
67. Ibid., 99.

More recently, she published a short study with the art historian Trần Kỳ Phương, comparing the cosmological dualism of contemporary Cham people with that of their ancestors in the ancient kingdom of Champa. The study emphasizes the relation between worship of the Hindu god Siva at Mỹ Sơn and the cult of the indigenous goddess Pô Nagar in the royal temple at Nha Trang. The authors identify a new set of opposing attributes and present them in a Dournes-style table (see table 4).[68]

Table 4. Elements of Siva worship and Pô Nagar worship

Siva (at Mỹ Sơn)	Pô Nagar (at Nha Trang)
male	female
Bhadresvara/Siva	Bhagavati/Parvati/Pô Yang Inu Nagar
mountain	sea
father	mother
north	south
valley	riverside hill near estuary

Various kings of Champa are recorded as having restored temples and made offerings at both temples. Applying Nakamura's findings about contemporary Cham cosmology, the two authors conclude that dedications made "to the two royal sanctuaries in the North as well as in the South of the kingdom suggests that [the kings] worshipped both the god and goddess in order to protect the whole kingdom. This reflected the co-existence of dualist states/clans and manifested the cosmological dualist cult."[69]

Comparison of this idea with Dournes's work suggests that Cham and Jarai cosmologies contained similar principles of complementary dualism. In both cases, complementary dualism acted as a mechanism for the maintenance of community identity when faced with the challenge of difference. For the Cham, it allowed the peaceful integration of outside religious elements, with the importation of Siva worship into indigenous

68. Trần Kỳ Phương and Nakamura, *Mỹ Sơn*, 18.
69. Ibid.

belief systems (in ancient Champa), then of Islam, along with its junction with Hinduism (in the more recent Balamon-Bani relationship). Meanwhile, for the Jarai, it ensured internal communal cohesion and harmonious political relations with the Cham, and later the Khmer, Việt, and other outsiders. For the Cham, complementary dualism was a tool for acculturation. For the Jarai, it allowed them to distinguish themselves from the powerful inhabitants of the coast while maintaining a place in the broader Champa community. The two models varied in their details but in both cases helped preserve a sense of common identity through mutual respect of differences. Seeing in complimentary dualism a powerful tool for communication and bonding between the respective groups, I wondered whether it could be added to Dournes's list of permanent institutions shared by the Cham and Jarai.

At this point, I started pondering the origins of this shared institution. Nakamura noted that all these terms (*ahier, awar, akafir*) are of Arabic origin. Complementarity between male and female principles, and their corresponding gods or aspects of those gods, may be observed in Hindu religion. Dournes's short survey of other forms of the Potao institution suggests that it was common among Southeast Asia's indigenous peoples.[70] Or should we regard the cosmology of complementary dualism as something broader, something shared by humanity as a whole (with its East Asian expression, for example, found in yin and yang)? I realized I had no way of answering any of these questions.

With this thought, I retreated. Perhaps, for the moment, I should ignore Dournes's anti-economic tirades, remember that the "economic" and the "cultural" were two sides of the same coin, stay focused on my study of Champa-highlander trade, and gracefully accept his posthumous "pfzz!"

Conclusion

After my successive readings, what can I say about the Potao, the Jarai, and ancient Champa in the hills?

---

70. See *PUT*, ch. 10, appendix, 288–92.

Firstly, theoretical definitions of the Potao institution are scattered through the book. Whether we are speaking of the king of fire, water, or wind, we see the Potao functioning as mediator with the Lord of Heaven (*PUT*, 287) and as the guardian of traditional order on earth (*PUT*, 193). He is the keystone to a social system, foundation of an ethnic community's identity (*PUT*, ch. 10B). He appears too as a "fictive" king, whose diplomatic skills and sharp sense of humor allows him to create equal alliances with empires. And as a political force at home, he harmonizes the people with each other, with the gods, and with nature. As Dournes described the king of fire, "the ritual Potao apui is the mythical anti-Potao, he is Rit, tousled and shaggy-haired, the little people resisting all oppression from outside, the ally of the forces of nature, the guardian of the order of the seasons, of the succession of dry and rain on which farming and the country's life depend" (*PUT*, 200).

Secondly, constitutional similarities between the Jarai and the Cham are manifested in arrangements of complementary dualism. Was this evidence of indirect Indianization of the Jarai? Or was it another aspect of the indigenous cultural "base" in Southeast Asia, which predated the Indianization of Champa, identified by Paul Mus?[71] Dournes seems to have shared Mus's view. But his comment on Indianization also offers food for thought. "Indianization formed Champa and Kambuja [Cambodia] from their original indigenous populations, of which a fraction accepted influence from India and the others gravitated more or less around these two powers constituted as states or maintained between them a tranquil independence" (*PUT*, 108).

As they gravitated around the Cham and Khmer centers, did the Jarai adopt elements of their Indianized cosmology? Did they employ elements of that cosmology to maintain politico-diplomatic relations with their powerful neighbors? This hypothesis is convincing in the light of the Potao foundation myths (*PUT*, ch. 7): the institution was created through political and military contact with superior powers, from Rit's successful struggle against the tyrant, adopting the name while rejecting the substance

---

71. Mus, "Cultes indiennes," 367–410.

of his defeated enemy's regime. This may also provide explanation for the memory that, unlike other Jarai, the Potao was cremated (*PUT*, 265–67).[72] Was this a sign of Indianized "civilized behavior," which—like the king of Siam's clothes—elicited the respect of powerful neighbors, guaranteeing the independence of the Jarai.[73]

Dournes rejects this hypothesis. If the Potao was indeed cremated, and this was not proved, it cannot have been a result of Cham *influence* (*PUT*, 265). For him, the Cham and Jarai were so close that they denied the very premise of "cultural influence." He presents much evidence to demonstrate this. His book's frontispiece underlines the physical resemblance of the ancient Cham people with today's Jarai (*PUT*, frontispiece and p. 94). According to Dournes, Cham and Jarai never name each other: Cham inscriptions mention outsiders, including other highlanders, but never speak of Jarai (*PUT*, 94). Sre and Koho myths identify the tyrant *potao* as Cham, while for the Jarai these tyrants were not outsiders (*PUT*, 154, 158, 160). While the Cham established authentic diplomatic relations with the Khmer (*PUT*, 101–4), the Cham-Jarai relation was of the type "town rat–field rat" (*PUT*, 99). For the Cham, "the Jarai were just an inferior social class who buried their dead because they lacked both the means to pay the high costs of a cremation and the clergy necessary to hold the rite" (*PUT*, 265).

Dournes's ideas on this subject are not fully developed. They sneak out of the book in snippets and asides. At several points, he states that the Jarai were non-Indianized Cham (*PUT*, 94, 142) or palaeo-Cham (*PUT*, 19, 265). Then, elsewhere, he adds that they later formed the "debris" of the ancient Cham kingdoms, "the heirs of Champa, perhaps more so (geographically at least) than the few Cham who live on the coast" (*PUT*, 19). By this time, he has clearly abandoned the thesis put forward in his

---

72. It should be noted that Dournes's ethnographic material did not allow him to be certain that, in the past, the Potao was cremated. He had evidence but noted that it was inconclusive.

73. The nineteenth-century kings of Siam adopted the European trappings of royalty, using their mastery of Western culture to appear civilized to the powerful intruder, to guarantee their kingdom's independence. See Peleggi, *Lords of Things*, 3.

first books (see box 2) that Champa established a system of state rule in the hills.

After reading *Pötao, une théorie*, I too am convinced there was no such system of direct rule. Between the isolationist tendencies of the Mạ, the loose networks of contacts operated by other groups, and the highly structured Potao system of the Jarai (*PUT*, 135), different highlanders evolved different ways of relating to lowland Champa. The most important of these must have been a complex network of alliances: the Potao, we now know, were masters of alliance. These ways of relating also included internecine raiding (*PUT*, 96), trade in forest products (*PUT*, 120), and the travel that served these and other purposes. Control of Potao country meant control of the passes between the Bình Định/Phú Yên region of Champa and the Stung Treng/Champassak sector of the Mekong. For both the Khmer and Cham, relations with the Jarai were essential for their role as "guardians of the trails" (*PUT*, 104). Dournes's comments on the complementary duality of the kings of fire and water, territorially expressed in their geographical location on either side of the watershed, emphasize the importance of this role.

> One can see how close to the [watershed] line the two Potao are located, almost equidistant, one on either side; this is the impact on the ground of the play of conjunction/disjunction between Water and Fire, opposing and complementary. They are like two people who turn their backs on the mountain ridge to look downstream. . . .
>
> The broken lines [on the map] indicate the main communication trails of the Jarai. The line of the ridge is not a barrier: over a distance of less than ten kilometers, it is broken by three major trails. The main axis of relations in ancient times was oriented east-west (today travel is almost entirely made in a north-south direction along roads): this is a representation on the ground of what is formed by the Potao through their function of relation making. (*PUT*, 273)

Thinking about the complexity of these relations, I returned to the map on page 95 of Dournes's book. Across the page, Dournes comments on our knowledge of the ancient past (*PUT*, 94): "We know little of the earliest Champa, not even where it was located." In Champa's later years, the brick towers—so beautifully illustrated on the map—stood as landmarks along a network of river-forest trails across the highlands. Was it because Cham-Jarai relations were under strain that travel required the creation of permanent stage posts? Or did it, by contrast, represent a rapprochement or development in those relations? Or did these buildings mark a Cham retreat into the hills and their demographic expansion there, as territories were lost to the north? Dournes does not speculate.

Better understanding Henri Maitre's despair at these questions (see p. 30–31), I turned to Dournes's photograph of the king of fire (*PUT*, opposite p. 144). The plateaus will keep some of their secrets, are his eyes saying? I remembered that, to obtain the knowledge presented in his book, Dournes spent long years in Jarai country. The photograph is of Rit—you can see it. Potao is Rit. Today, after reading *Pötao, une théorie*, that insight is enough.

Postscript

Dournes worked hard to understand the montagnard–Champa relationship. He also admitted the story was unfinished. His article on highland Champa opens with the words, "It is not possible to fix the frontiers of Champa," and warns against the drawing of "Cartesian" lines. He planned to investigate the question through archaeological survey. In the 1960s, however, war limited his access to the field. Then in 1970, he was obliged to leave Vietnam.[74]

Archaeology may yield some answers (although several highland Champa sites surveyed by Parmentier have now disappeared). Many historical sources, especially in Cham, remain unread. We may learn more through anthropological research. At the same time, for those wishing to continue the work he started, Dournes proposed we ask not about borders, but a much more general question: "What was happening in the country's interior at the time of the Cham empire, in the broad sense of a zone of political-cultural influence located somewhere between the Mekong and the sea?"[75]

---

74. Dournes, "Recherches," 143, 144, 148.
75. Ibid., 143.

The research and the story it tells is unfinished. But even an unfinished story may have a postscript. The postscript to this one came a month after I wrote the conclusion above, recognizing Rit in the Potao's photograph. During fieldwork with Hrê people in Quảng Ngãi province,[76] we had just finished lunch. As the last drops of rice vodka gave way to cups of green tea, the district official with us that day, a young Hrê, asked: "Do we have any knowledge of the location of the western borders of Champa?"

I could hardly repeat Dournes's warning about the irrelevance of borderlines. Yet how, in a few minutes, could I satisfy his curiosity about this question to which the answers are so few and so blurred? My colleague Nguyễn Tiến Đông replied first. An archaeologist, he described the brick towers on the plateaus. While there were no borders, he said, at the very least these vestiges testify to a late Cham presence in the hills. I added my view of Champa as a socioeconomic system that embraced the highlands. Networks of economic exchange and a hierarchy based on social rankings linked the various populations living in the hills and plains.

These answers provoked another question. "How did Champa's political system operate?" My colleague answered with comments about Champa kingship and Champa's capacity to attack the Đại Việt capital at Thăng Long. I developed this by saying, "If we're thinking about Champa and the highlands, we should also consider the way montagnard societies functioned. Montagnard politics were about *making alliances*. We can describe montagnard politics with three main points. Firstly, in the Central Highlands, the political unit was the village, independent of higher authority. Secondly, periodic conflicts erupted between villages. Thirdly, inhabitants and villages held ceremonies to create alliances. The Cham couldn't rule over such a society. Rather, we must imagine that they participated in this system, that they too made alliances with different montagnard groups."

Saying this, I thought of Dournes's book. It occurred to me to add that "the Jarai, when they invented the institution of the Potao, may have perfected a system of creating and maintaining alliances with the

---

76. Ba Động commune, Ba Tơ district, March 2009.

Andrew Hardy and Nguyễn Tiến Đông in after-lunch discussion with locals, Ba Động commune, Ba Tơ district, Quảng Ngãi province (2009)

rulers of Champa. The Potao system itself may have emerged from such a relationship." But I thought too of the time it would take to tell the Potao story, the way my Vietnamese language skills would falter in the telling, and the fieldwork we had to do in the afternoon. I let the thought go.

So what did it actually mean to say that the highlands were part of Champa?[77]

As Dournes saw, the Cham and Jarai shared a common ethnolinguistic origin: "The Cham are just Jarai who were Indianized and then, some of them, Islamized."[78] The Cham and Jarai operated a single economic system, maintained through trade and travel, sourcing products in the highlands, exporting from coastal ports. But we cannot assume that these commonalities were the basis for a unified political entity.

Champa itself was politically fragmented, its system based on fluctuating alliances. Also fragmented, the Jarai too used alliances in their

77. See Lafont, *Le Campa*.
78. Dournes, "Recherches," 157.

political relationships, operating mainly at the village level.[79] My reading of Dournes suggested that the Jarai may have participated in the Champa political system, making and breaking alliances with lords and kings (the *potao*-lords of Jarai legends) through their supra-village institution, the Potao (the sacred *potao* figure Rit, not a king but happy to appear as one).

The legends in Dournes's book suggest that this institution emerged to give a political identity to the Jarai in their dealings with outside powers, to provide them with an interlocutor with royalty. This was the way the Potao institution worked during the post-Champa period, in Jarai relations with the Khmer and Viet kingdoms. The Potao institution allowed the Jarai to have close relations with the lowland kingdoms of Champa while maintaining an ethnic and political identity apart.

Such a system of Potao-mediated, alliance-based politics between Champa and the Jarai must have predated the construction of Sivaite temple-towers along the main trading routes between Champa on the coast and Champassak on the Mekong. Thus for our understanding of the Cham-Jarai relationship, the archaeological evidence in the hills may well turn out to represent a red herring. The highland towers were built during the late period of Champa, in the fourteenth and fifteenth centuries. They might even mark a new development in the relationship between the Cham and the Jarai. Did their construction correspond to a period when Indianized Cham from the plains decided for the first time— under pressure from the Vietnamese to the north—to establish a more permanent presence in the hills?

Many questions remain. But I now realized that an understanding of the politics of highland Champa was not only to be found in the book *Pötao, une theorie*. It lay in the Potao institution itself.

---

79. On the "decentralized, if not fragmented" politics of the montagnards and the existence of supra-village organizations, including the Potao, see Salemink, *Ethnography*, 34–35.

PART 2

The Vietnamese and Highlanders in the Twentieth Century: Interview with Jacques Dournes

JD – Nowadays people no longer do *thèses d'état*.[1] They do university theses! It's not difficult to do a thesis. You submit whatever rubbish you choose to a committee of examiners who knows nothing at all about it. You are the only one who understands the issue, and you leave with the top grade. Not complicated. All you need is a supervisor who's willing to play along.

But I can boast of a *thèse d'état* at the Sorbonne, with Lévi-Strauss on the committee. There was a crowd in the Sorbonne lecture theater. It was packed. I had a great laugh. Of all the committee members, Lévi-Strauss was the only one who had read my thesis, and the only one with whom I conversed. He attacked me on issues of structural analysis. He attacked me, I replied, it was ping pong. It was brilliant in every respect, magnificent. That was the twenty-third of June, 1973. That's nearly twenty years ago. I was already old! Fifty years old. In those days, it was rare to submit a *thèse d'état* before you were fifty. I submitted mine a year after Condominas, a

This interview was conducted by the author on February 1–2, 1992, in Bagard, France. This edited and condensed transcript was published in the original French in *Aséanie* 24 (December 2009), 149–71. A fuller version of the transcript in French is published here in the appendix.

1. The *doctorat d'état* (state doctorate) was a higher-level doctorate in the French academic system.

year after Haudricourt and several others.[2] So I was one of the youngest to submit a *thèse d'état*. At that time, it was a serious matter.

AH – And Gourou's thesis, *Les paysans du delta*, was that a *thèse d'état*?[3]

JD – For me, it's currently the work of reference. Gourou was a good fellow, a straight man, perfectly straight. I am not a geographer. I don't know Tonkin, what people called Tonkin in those days and later called North Vietnam. But it seems to me nonetheless difficult to talk about the peasants of the delta and only deal with the subject of farming. There are the people too, what they do in their house, their language. And Gourou, he didn't speak Vietnamese and [never knew what it was to] get his bare feet wet in the paddy fields.

That's where I'm at. If one hasn't been barefoot in the paddy fields, one knows nothing, because everything happens in people's heads. Economics, agronomics, these are epiphenomena, and they don't explain the phenomena. Whether it's Gourou for Tonkin, Delvert for Cambodia, or many others, they have not been wet in the mud.[4] They are sociologists. There are figures, there are yields per hectare, stuff like that. For me, that's of no interest (though I don't say that for economists it is not). What interests me is people in relation to their milieu: what they do with it, what they make of it, diachronically, through the centuries and through the evolution of people's politics and psychology—how people, barefoot in the paddy fields with mud halfway up their legs, reflect, react, think, and dream of other things too. That's what's interesting. Yields per hectare, I don't give a damn, I've never measured that. I'm an anthropologist, I'm not a geographer.

[Discussion about choosing a thesis subject.]

You talk to me about dates [regarding the subject of your thesis]. You talk to me about 1950 to 1960. That doesn't correspond to anything. You know

2. André-Georges Haudricourt: like Georges Condominas, a renowned anthropologist.

3. Gourou, Pierre, *Les paysans du delta Tonkinois : étude de géographie humaine* (Paris: Mouton, 1965).

4. Jean Delvert: geographer and author of *Le paysan cambodgien* (Paris: Imprimerie Nationale, 1961).

very well that the dates of history are not the dates of the centuries. The twentieth century started in 1919 and the twenty-first century started in 1991. It's human events that make the epochs, dates, and sequences. So for Indochina, if you want to take a slice, [you should choose] 1946–54—a little historical job that no one dares to tackle openly.

AH – The Indochina war . . .

JD – No! It was during the Americans' time that there was war. I'm talking about the French time. I know it completely. I disembarked in Indochina in 1946 and I was kicked out in 1954! I know it completely, from every side: the French side, the Vietnamese side, the minorities' side. And I can guarantee you that from 1946 to 1954, people weren't doing war. War, the war started in 1954.

AH – What were they doing?

JD – It was . . . it was comedy. Comedy! The French wanted to make money, and people were cheating on all sides.

You also need to know all the history of what happened just before 1946. From 1940 to 1945 French Indochina was under the sway of Admiral Decoux, Pétainist *à bloc*, like all those heads of provinces, those bishops, all the French.[5] Indochina was Pétainist and pro-German. By consequence, not hostile to the Japanese.

In 1945, the Japanese coup in Indochina. Decoux and company were totally cuckolded: the Japs took power, put the French into concentration camps, and had the brilliant idea of giving the Vietnamese their independence. Vietnam's independence came through the grace of the Mikado! It's historically true!

In 1946, De Gaulle decided on the military re-conquest of Indochina. So, in spring–summer 1946, several ships full of soldiers left Marseille for Saigon, for the re-conquest. I was on the first civilian boat, in September–October 1946, so I'm absolutely contemporary to events.

At that time [December 1946], Ho Chi Minh, who was not a rogue, said, "Let the French send us teachers, but not soldiers!" I heard him. Youngster that I was—I was twenty-four—I declared in full assembly of

---

5. Philippe Pétain (1856–1951): a general, and Vichy France's head of state from 1940–44.

all those priests, bishops, administrators, and all that: "Ho Chi Minh is right. French culture but no battle." Oh, I showed myself up right from the start! Ho Chi Minh never knew anything about it, but I got it right in the teeth. He was right: it's a fact that today there is not one Vietnamese who speaks French in Vietnam.

What's more, that De Gaulle appointed as governor general Thierry d'Argenlieu—a [defrocked] Carmelite monk whom we also called Ruolz, because Ruolz is the brand name of a type of fork used as a substitute for silverware [*argenterie*]. He was a complete laughing stock, Thierry d'Argenlieu.

AH – Did d'Argenlieu send many of the Indochina Pétainists back to France?

JD – Pretty much all of them. Even the bishop of Saigon, the last French bishop of Saigon, who was head of the Pétainist Legion in Indochina, that is, head of all the Pétainist French!

[Pause]

I'll give you a generality about economic life. It's that throughout the French period—the period of the wicked colonialists, the one that I knew from 1946 to 1954—everyone ate well. You could travel on the roads, the train from Saigon to Hanoi ran normally, and the people ate well. Oh . . . there were skirmishes in the bush, [the Viet Minh] against the French, against I know not what. But they were skirmishes, nothing more.

Vietnam is a truly rich country. I never saw anyone go hungry, even during the American war. Except in the concentration camps, because the Americans built concentration camps not only for the Vietnamese, the so-called communists, but also for the ethnic minorities, for the highlanders (the Moi)—and there people died of starvation abundantly. But in the villages—I had forty or so villages within a radius of ten kilometers around my house, a very rich valley—I never saw anyone go hungry, never!

Vietnam used to export rice, yes, whereas since the American period Vietnam has imported rice from Thailand. That says a lot. And why?

Because Hanoi's Stalinist empire requisitioned all the rice to send it to Russia, under the pretext that the Russians had helped the Vietnamese to get their independence. War debt! But above all because during the American period the tanks, the few Vietnamese tanks, the few Vietnamese planes, all their arms, were entirely Russian. The funny thing is that those arms transited through China, though the Chinese detested the Russians but closed their eyes. The Vietnamese sent all their rice to Russia, up to Gorbachev's time. Result: no more rice for the Vietnamese peasants.

Since the departure of the French, but especially after 1975—it was after 1975 that things became catastrophic in Vietnam. That was when the boat people left. The Hanoi regime had reunified Vietnam. By contrast with Korea [for example], this was by no means historically obvious. The Korea problem was entirely political and American—there were never two Koreas in history. It's like Germany. By contrast, Vietnam has always had its northern and southern kingdoms. And they've never liked each other. They have dialects such that someone from Hanoi and someone from Saigon have difficulty understanding each other, not to mention people from Huế, who speak yet another dialect. It's a matter of where you put the accents, the tones. They only just understand each other. On the telephone, they don't understand each other at all. They have to write if they want to understand.

So after 1975, the Hanoi regime imposed its structures, notably economic structures. There was no more private property. All the workers gave everything to the state. The state gave them three baubles for three hundred tonnes. It was the same as what happened in Russia, which is an extremely rich country. Russia is a land of plenty. It's stupid to send food aid at the moment, as long as it's not being distributed, for the very good reason that there is no distribution network. You have to ask this bureau, who will ask that bureau, who will ask this bureau, and between one bureau and the next there's always a loafer who has forgotten to make the phone call, and it remains like that for months—while the potatoes rot, etc., etc. The regime—that's what it's like.

Outraged at no longer having private property, outraged at having to give everything to the state, the Vietnamese peasants, and the highlanders too, produced less and less. Result: they had nothing to eat. The rich imported rice from Thailand, whereas it was the other way around when I was in Vietnam.

[Pause]

AH – Did the Indochina war have a big impact on the economy?

JD – One should distinguish the French war from the American war. The French war was to defend a colony—a settlement colony—something the Americans have never done. French people, entire families—planters—settled and stayed there for decades. They were interested in the country. They loved the land, they put down roots, sometimes with a Vietnamese woman, and it didn't work badly at all.

It wasn't as terrible as all that—colonial rule. Oh, there were prisons, Poulo Condore—a few dozen guys who got themselves called communist and packed off to prison—but there weren't any horrible scenes.[6] At the economic level, the French had plantations—rubber, tea, coffee—which only benefited the Europeans. Because the Vietnamese didn't use that rubber, didn't drink coffee, and already had plenty of tea. The plantations were only there for the French planters' profits.

AH – And the people who worked—the Vietnamese?

JD – Most were from the North. Because in the South, there are plenty of paddy fields, the rich paddy fields of Cochinchina. So they worked in the paddy fields. There was a surplus of rice. People sold it everywhere. I have always known Vietnam as an exporter of rice. But they needed coolies on the plantations and, as the highlanders—it's their character, they are anarchists!—didn't want to work for a boss, they brought Vietnamese down from the North. And they worked well.

AH – Did they benefit?

JD – They weren't unhappy. They were paid, they were fed, they were housed—they weren't unhappy. There was a sort of shop on the plantation

---

6. Poulo Condore or Côn Đảo Island: a penitentiary off the coast of southern Vietnam.

where they could buy, deducted from their salary, clothes, tobacco, knickknacks. They didn't have money like in the village.

AH – They couldn't go and shop at the market?

JD – The plantations were a long way from the town centers. They were in the bush. There was no public transport. Once the poor Vietnamese coolie from the North settled there, he didn't move any further. They themselves were the market!

AH – But in 1945, after the coup, they all abandoned the plantations.

JD – There weren't many northerners in 1945. No, it started after 1946. Before that, there were small family businesses, no very large ones, other than Michelin. But Michelin, that was rubber and it was on the border between Vietnam and Cambodia. In fact, the biggest plantations were in Cambodia, Mondolkiri province. The plantations developed between 1946 and 1954. Huge development! I saw it. From day to day, I saw the progress. I saw the French planters, gun in hand, going into my villages, forcing my... Moi to go and work on their plantations. I complained. The French administrator backed me up. He was ousted, sent to Africa. And me, a few years afterwards, I was ousted. Because the planters, the Bank of Indochina and Bảo Đại—they were all the same thing! I was called the "red priest" by Bảo Đại. He had me repatriated.

So, the Vietnamese from the North arrived on the plantations. They built their houses, put down roots, and they're still there. The plantations are theirs now, with a Chinese contribution, one mustn't forget. The owner, of course, is Chinese. It was the Chinese who replaced the French as the big plantation owners.

AH – Are they still Chinese now? After 1978–79?

JD – I don't have information on that. But while I was still there, the Chinese were the big bosses and the northern Vietnamese worked, not unhappily at all. All that made Vietnam's wealth: tea, coffee, rubber. Especially tea and coffee—[the price of] rubber regularly fell, because people made synthetic rubber, quite simply. Tea and coffee worked really well, in economic terms.

As for the highlanders, when people left them in peace, they ate well! Think about it. On the high plateaus—my dear country—the density was eight to the square kilometer, while in Hanoi, the density was eighty to ninety to the square kilometer! It was luxury! You scratched the soil a bit, sowed a few grains of rice, and harvested loads, loads, loads of it—and good rice at that! People ate really well. There were no problems.

AH – And in the southern delta?

JD – In the Mekong Delta, a very, very rich land, they had three rice harvests a year. It's packed with alluvium: it flows down, flows down . . . it'll clog up the sea. In the end Indochina will join up with Malaysia if it carries on like that. In two thousand years, maybe that'll happen.

[Pause]

There were two economies. One was the internal economy. That is, how the people lived, the Vietnamese peasants like the highlander peasants: small family farms, an ultra-rich soil. I'm talking about before 1954, during the so-called French war. I could go to the house of any peasant. I was fed like that. I had a feast! Little fish, crabs from the paddy fields, all sorts of delicious things, real fish sauce! The Vietnamese peasant and the highlander are enormously alike. They have never been enemies (people have invented things about that). It was dog-eat-dog, that yes! But it worked very well. There were no fights, there were no battles, there was nothing.

So much for the internal economy. As for the external economy, there were substantial exports—tea, coffee, rubber—and they earned vast quantities of foreign exchange for Vietnam. So it was all very balanced.

AH – Did the Vietnamese have an important role in that economy?

JD – Mainly the Chinese.

AH – The Vietnamese, they were . . .

JD – Executors. Up to 1954, everyone lived well. In every house there was enough to eat every day and feed ten kids. Yes, I say ten kids—that was the average for a family. I have statistics on that for the Jarai. Average births: ten per marriage. Survivors: seven, after three years. Not bad, eh? Which meant that the Vietnamese, who barely numbered forty million in 1946, are now ninety million, many more than the French on a much smaller territory. You can understand why they invaded Laos and Cambodia. Whenever an American shot down a Vietnamese during the war, a Vietnamese woman brought two kids into the world. It was sunk in advance, America's military policy. They give birth, give birth, give birth, and everyone works. At the age of four, the kid starts working in the garden. They farm the streams, the edges of paths—they farm everything. They grow sweet potatoes, chilli peppers, peanuts—they grow everything right up to the edge of the road. They are indefatigable workers, the Vietnamese, tireless. For that, for their work, I respect them. How they work!

You only have to look in Paris: the boat people, they arrive in the 13th District without a dime. They start by doing the washing up in a Vietnamese restaurant. That lasts six months, maximum. After that they wait on tables. After that they help with the cooking. And in less than a year, they open a restaurant next door. They make their fortune. Bravo for their work. And what's more, what they make is good. It's healthy, it's fresh, it's good, it's clean. No one has ever been sick from a Vietnamese dish. The Vietnamese have made their place here. I once heard a Vietnamese trader in Paris, Place Maubert, say to me: "Ah Paris, it's our finest colony!" Is that not beautiful? They colonize France in their turn, with plenty of humor and plenty of friendship for France. A fine turn of the tables, without a struggle, nothing violent, they just made their place through their work and its quality.

So you see, the internal family economy worked very well, as long as it was anarchy. Because the French never checked what was going on in the villages. Hanoi was far away and paid little attention to the South. So practically speaking it was what's called Vietnamese "communism," that is, [the predominance] of the commune. It was perfect in those days. Everyone has very good memories of it. Because the French didn't really want to fight.

When I was young, I was like my little dog. I went snooping, I went everywhere—I was in the military camps, in the encampments, in the little forts lost deep in the forest. I saw godforsaken Frenchmen, three or four at a time, with a few highlanders around them. Terribly frightened, they dared not leave their fort. They were supplied by helicopter, ha! They didn't want to fight! It took some absurd generals to want to organize a great battle in northern Vietnam, to retake an Indochina that had already escaped them.

AH – Still they wanted to defend their economic interests.

JD – Not the military, they didn't give a damn about that. The military and the planters couldn't set eyes on one another. Bah! There was no French collusion there, none at all.

AH – And the industrialists, the planters, how did they cope?

JD – Absolutely fine! No one went to their plantations. From time to time, the Viet Minh turned up to shoot a poor coolie to scare people. Nothing much, up to 1954. Trifles. No, it wasn't really war. The French planters were very happy.

AH – Did they think they'd stay?

JD – Yes, everyone thought they'd stay. Me too. Well . . . they had their enemies, I had mine, but everyone thought they'd stay.

AH – And the Chinese in all that?

JD – Oh, the Chinese, in the interior, nothing much. Up to 1954, it wasn't yet developed. But they controlled the import-export trade in Saigon.

AH – How did the rice get from the fields to Chợ Lớn?[7]

JD – It depends on when. Up to 1954, there was domestic consumption and there was the Chinese buyer who collected the surplus and went to sell it at the port of Saigon. He lived at Chợ Lớn and had some small Chinese who worked for him, who went and did the buying.

AH – So there was a whole network.

JD – Yes, all that was networks. What people called the Chinese congregations. That's funny too, the fact that in their house all those Chinese—who weren't for Chiang Kai Shek and still less for Mao Tse Tung—had a portrait of Sun Yat Sen, the common father of both branches. It's delightful!

Tea, coffee, rice, everything for sale was thus shipped to Saigon and kept in large warehouses run by the Chinese. When a particular merchandise

7. The Chinese market district of Saigon.

started running short, the Chinese closed the warehouse and the prices rose and rose . . . then they opened it and sold [at high prices]!

In 1955–56, I saw a masterstroke with the Chinese traders in the little village of Choreo, in Jarai country. When I arrived, there was no one there but the Jarai village, my house on the outskirts, the road, and a few Vietnamese traders. A few Jarai tried to do a bit of trade. Knickknacks and trifles: canned food, matches, etc. But it didn't work at all, because the Jarai are philosophers, artists, poets. They bought something for one piaster, and wanted to sell it for two to make money immediately. As for the Vietnamese, they just about got by.

Then some Chinese arrived. For one or two months, they sold at loss— what cost them two piasters, they sold for one—and in two months they had completely sunk the Vietnamese and controlled the market. After that, they put the prices up as they wished. Three years later, there was a Chinese school at Choreo in front of the village, for all the Chinese children there. That's the Chinese: knowing how to sell at loss to sink the competition. They succeeded, they sank everyone. The Vietnamese, the Jarai, they sank them all. They had their congregation in Saigon [so they had the necessary capital for such maneuvers].

International trade worked in the same way. That was when there were still freighters—mainly French, Italian, sometimes English—maybe one per year, which brought goods into the port of Saigon. That no longer exists. The Chinese bought the cargo before they knew what was in it. They bought the whole ship. The French wanted what was called the bill of lading: to know what was on board, and then to buy this part or that part of it. The Chinese—the wealthy fat Chinese, the lover of Marguerite Duras—turned up and said, "Me, I'll buy the lot, the lot!" He knew very well that it was all perfectly marketable. Because freighters of that size didn't transport garbage. The cargo went to the Chinese warehouses in Chợ Lớn. When demand for a particular product began to rise, the Chinese sold in small quantities. And when it started running short, bingo! They sold at exorbitant prices. They made some filthy fortunes— that was something no Vietnamese could do.

AH – Because the Vietnamese had the same idea as the Jarai?

JD – Yes, small immediate profits. Because in the end the Vietnamese and the highlanders—I'm talking about the peasants, the people of the interior, I'm not talking about the bourgeois, the city people—they are very similar, psychologically. Culturally completely different, but psychologically they are small farmers of small plots of land. They help each other out, there are no big problems, no racial animosity, no. The racists, they call the savages on the high plateaus, my friends, *Moi*. What the Greeks called the *barbaroi*.

AH – What trade between villages was there?

JD – It depends. Between Vietnamese, nothing much, because they harvest the same things on their small farms: a few vegetables, garden produce, fruit trees. On the other hand, among the highlanders, the Moi, the Jarai, the Sre and company, it's completely specialized. Some do pottery, some do basket making, some do weaving. Some do metalwork, because iron ore—they forge it very well. And they trade. It circulates up there all the time, all the time.

AH – And who was doing the trade?

JD – Private individuals. There were no Chinese. It was one individual to another.

AH – So there were no traders?

JD – Not at all! Not at all!

AH – Did they use money?

JD – No. Barter! Money didn't exist. I'm talking about the high plateaus, eh!

AH – The distances were small?

JD – Oh, they could go more than a hundred kilometers! There were Jarai who went two hundred kilometers to give a buffalo to some Lao and get a jar or gong in exchange. Two hundred kilometers!

AH – Because they knew there were jars and gongs there?

JD – There aren't any in the Vietnamese part [of Indochina]. They're on the other side. They went great distances. All the highlanders from the high plateaus who went down to the coast—a hundred and fifty kilometers, along what were called the salt trails, all those trails that went roughly west-east, from the mountains to the coast—[bartered] rhinoceros horn, pigs, woven cloth for fish sauce, salt or salted fish, which they took home. It's been going on for centuries. It's extremely well known, narrated by many foreign scribblers, of course. It circulates a great deal, and it's all very amicable and friendly, dog-eat-dog (we're in Asia, and there are no notebooks, accounts, checks). It worked very well.

AH – How did they travel?

JD – On foot! If you travel with pigs at your heels, it takes less than a week from the high plateaus to the coast. If you do a forced march, it can take three days. A hundred and fifty kilometers. That's not too bad—I've done it.

AH – What shoes do they have?

JD – They don't have shoes. Nor do the Vietnamese, I'm talking about the country people. Everyone is barefoot. You keep to the trails. If you leave the trails, then you put on a type of small sandal made from a tire or something like that, because of the rattan. Rattan is a liana, thicker than a thumb, which runs along the ground with horrible thorns every ten centimeters. And if you step on a rattan thorn, [it hurts]! But on the trails you go barefoot. I'm still barefoot! I wonder how one can stuff one's feet into shoes that hurt so much. Feet are like hands, they start narrow and end broad. And shoes, they're quite the opposite, they start broad and end narrow. So, your foot in a shoe—it's completely absurd!

AH – Were there thieves?

JD – Yes. The Jarai in particular were known to be wonderful thieves. They stole horses. Never rice! It was sacred, you didn't have the right to touch it. The rice barns were outside the village, no one ever touched them. If rice was stolen, there'd have been a general outcry, there'd have been a killing, it would have been horrible. I have never heard of a case of rice theft. But otherwise, people stole, yes, people stole! Abundantly.

You see, I had a hut that didn't have a door. Sometimes I would leave for three or four days, on my rounds. Once or twice I deliberately left a few Vietnamese piasters in sight like that on my desk, which was on the ground. When I got back after four or five days, no one had touched anything. People had come in, just to do the dusting—friends who came to clean—yes! They saw it, they left it.

AH – And on the trails?

JD – Oh, we're not in China. There aren't any bandits, there aren't any pirates, there aren't any brigands, nothing on the trails. There might be tigers, at worst. Anyway, the tiger is such a coward. When he smells man, he clears off. He has to be really starving to attack. In general, there was no danger, never any attack. It's the calmest country in the world.

AH – Did the highlanders participate in the Vietnamese economy?

JD – Oh, very locally, at small markets. They took a basket of oranges to get a blouse in exchange, things like that. Obviously in the broader sense of the term, that's part of the economy, but it's very insignificant in Vietnamese commerce. In the past, it was more substantial, when there were no Europeans, no trade outside the Indochina peninsula. In those days the Vietnamese, who were only along the coast, traded a lot with the populations of the hinterland, who went down with pigs, elephant tusks, rhinoceros horns, cinnamon wood to get fish, fish sauce, things like that . . . That went on a great deal.

A bit later, there were Annamite peddlers—that's what they were called at the time—who came up to the plateaus to sell knickknacks in the villages. I've seen them.

At one point, completely in cahoots with the Viet Minh, the peddlers, who traveled everywhere, sold poisoned sweets, poisoned liquor. To liquidate them! Because all the Vietnamese on all sides, from Saigon, from Hanoi, from the maquis or from the government had only one idea: get rid of the highlanders. That lasted quite a long time. There were hundreds of deaths among the Jarai.

AH – When was that?

JD – In the years around 1968. I left in 1970.

[Pause]

JD – [One thing that would be interesting to] study is the Vietnamese economy, culturally Vietnamese as such, before the intrusion of foreigners.

What was the Vietnamese economy like before 1859? In general terms, there was the commune, the mandarins, and the emperor—a Confucian system. You need to know the economic dimension of Confucianism. It's not as obvious as that, but without it you can't understand anything about the Vietnamese economy before the intrusion of foreigners. And even then, because if the capture of Saigon was in 1859, there were French who turned up under Louis XIV, and before that there were Portuguese. [Certainly,] the French were useless at trade and good only for building Vauban forts, but the Portuguese were better at it. They must then—especially the Portuguese—have deeply changed the Vietnamese economy (opening ports, etc.).

You have to go back even further, to the twelfth century, roughly, with the arrival of the Arabs. A good part of Champa became Muslim. The coast was commercially colonized by the Arabs. That goes back a long way, that story does. So the Vietnamese economy—if there ever was one originally (because before that, it was Chinese)—was changed by all these foreign inputs. To manage all that, you really need to be an economist, a historian . . .

I can't tell you any more. I've told you all I know, which is nothing! It's not my problem, I've never worked on it.

AH – Was the only Vietnamese economy the village economy?

JD – You can study it at that level. Because, no more than the Chinese, the Arabs, and later on the Portuguese, the French didn't penetrate the villages. They contacted the mandarins, the emperors—the big bosses—but nothing at the village level. If it is true that Vietnam is a country of villages, the village economy may offer a key to understanding the victory of 1975: [you can destroy as many villages as you want], there is always another just nearby. It's like in the myths. You cut the serpent's head and it grows seven new ones. That is one of Vietnam's strengths, because despite all its appearances, its mandarins, its imperial system, its Confucianism, it is relatively anarchic: there is no higher power, everyone gets by in their corner. People didn't talk about the emperor, they didn't even know the mandarin. And the emperor was informed about nothing, nor was the mandarin—and he couldn't care less. For a rebellion, for the Viet Minh, this was a pearl, a real find. They played this card, and that's how they won. When a system like Hanoi's nationalist Stalinism can infiltrate this, it finds dots everywhere on the map where its troops can be resupplied. No one could thwart them through authority. The little village worked on a basis of anarchy.

It took a Vietnamese like Ho Chi Minh to sense it. It was truly brilliant and it worked. It should also be compared with other phenomena of Stalinist imperialism, as in Russia. Everyone got by in their little corner, there was no central authority. Minor secondary underlings [collected] taxes, which remained in the underlings' pockets, but the tsar was informed of nothing.

[Pause]

JD – What makes me a bit uncomfortable is not only that I'm not an economist—I know nothing about the economy—but that it doesn't interest me in the least. What interests me is culture, techniques, myths and people, the epics, all that people tell and that they can think. And what's more, I know nothing about the Vietnamese. I lived among them but I was in my shell: the Vietnamese, the war, I didn't give a damn. That the Vietnamese, the French, the Americans, the Chinese, the whoever were fighting each other, I was completely outside all that. I was exclusively a minorities guy.

My main interest was culture. I'm talking about the intellectual, religious, mystical, poetic values that you find in oral literature, myths, legends, poems. That's what I want to work on above all. The rest, I don't give a damn—that is my economy. Everything I've written about the populations with whom I lived and on whom I worked in the sense I've just told you: those are cultural values of universal character.

AH – But in their values, people still had an eye on economic matters. When we talk about the values of thought, people thought about earning their bread.

JD – In the area I know, literature, such thought did not exist. There's nothing to be found there, unless you get the texts to say what they're not saying. Nothing. It's drowsy-making, it's poetic, it's dreams, it's the other, it's great poetry! It's as though you asked me if there was an economic dimension to the Song of Roland. Or, worse, to the romance of the Grail: modern economics in the romance of the Grail, it's side-splitting!

AH – They aren't interested in everyday life, in fact.

JD – Not only are they not interested, they deliberately go elsewhere.

AH – To escape . . .

JD – It's not to escape. It's to have a laugh. An escape route, that means that one wants to flee something. There's nothing to flee. Everyday life, you live it—between dreams—but it's not a value. Rice is not a value. And cooking rice is not a value. It's a necessity, just like when you poo, no? Everyday I eat my rice, everyday I poo, everyday I eat my chilli. These things are mechanical, biological. No one cares. It's natural, it's simple, you don't talk about it, it's of no interest.

When you're free in the evening, at night, or when it's raining too much, and you can't go out, you drink! You invent a heap of fine things, the Holy Grail, the Song of Roland, Tristan and Isolde, etc. The economic side to all that? It's anti-economic. It's free. . . It's pure creation and creation is free by definition.

As for the economists . . . ! When I read *Le Monde* for example, I read the first page, sometimes the second, rarely the last. But when I see the three or four pages "Economy" in the middle, they go straight into the grate to light my fire. I am completely allergic to the economy. Because it's exactly the opposite of free—and literary creation is free. It's of no use, it doesn't earn a penny for all those people, the fact that they've invented extraordinary myths. In the Middle Ages, there were no royalties. The authors of Tristan and Isolde, the Grail Quest, King Arthur never received any royalties.

When I translate their myths and can publish them, I send them some cash. But they don't even think about it. They don't understand that having told a wonderful story might bring in some cash. For me, it's to thank them, because I've never paid an informant. I didn't have informants, I had friends. I've never given a penny to anyone. What's more, over there I didn't have a penny—and now that's started up again, I don't have a penny now. While I was at the CNRS, I just about got by, I published. So from time to time, I tried to pay my debts, to send. They didn't understand! It's free, you don't pay for something that's free! It's an insult, almost. I give you a gift and you give me some money in exchange for my gift. A storyteller who told me a wonderful epic that lasted four or five hours, it would be an insult to give anything at all. It's a gush of freedom.

So I am anti-economic just as I am an anarchist! I am a comedian, you know. I know very well that I'm playing comedy. I do it deliberately, I know what I'm doing. It amuses me and at the same time, there's something in it.

Economics and money, don't talk to me about it. I'm on the other side, right over on the other side. And that doesn't come from my cultural roots: I am the son of a bourgeois and had a lot of money. It came from contact with the savages. It was they who cultivated me. Yes! They taught me values I didn't know. You can be in the mud of the rice field, you can be doing dumb work that you don't like, you have to eat. And then there's a moment when it comes and you are free and you are yourself and you are inventing, you are creating, you are making poems. They showed me that: that you can create, get out of your shit, even as you stay within it. And that's very strong.

For me, these populations have greater appeal. They're killing them, of course. They do all they can to kill them. They are so afraid of creation, because creation is anarchic by definition. You create, so you go outside the norms, so it's anarchic, so they suppress it. Vietnam is doing it with their minorities and Russia did it with millions of people as far as the very depths of Siberia, liquidating them and replacing them with Slavs. If you speak of Amazonians—dear Christopher Columbus, he was not responsible. He was . . . like Boudarel![8] He set out with a false ideal:

Rovers and captains out of Palos rose,
To daring, brutish dreams mad to the core.[9]

They are not like other people, they are inventing, they are artists. By suppressing them, people suppress all those who have the nerve, the

---

8. Georges Boudarel (1926–2003): French academic accused in 1991 of torturing French prisoners for the Viet Minh during the Indochina war.

9. Dournes cites two lines of José Maria de Heredia's sonnet "The Conquerors," referring to Columbus's voyage, published in *Sonnets of José-Maria de Heredia*, trans. Edward Robeson Taylor (San Francisco: W. Doxey, 1897), 113.

cheek, the daring to want to create, to go out—not to escape—to go out, to go up, to go and see other things.

You see, in a Jarai village, fifteen or so people in the hut, it's spontaneous. A storyteller starts an epic. He is expressing "a thought that has not yet been thought" which was a bit in everyone's mind and which he brings to the surface like that, through his organ: his voice! He's a comedian, a storyteller. And the organ, you have to hear it. I have recordings of such beauty, through the language, through the organ, which charms. And he speaks what is underneath, inside, what is in all the hearts of all those present, the kids just like the old folk. After an hour of the tale, the kids fall asleep, because there are no children's tales, no old folk's tales. Everyone is there, everyone takes what they can. The kids fall asleep, the old folk a bit later, the women last of all: they are tough, they don't sleep much. There are women storytellers too. It's extraordinary.

That's what I call the economy of those populations. I completely reverse the problem, deliberately. That is their economy. It's still going on. I left them twenty-two years ago. They are still writing to me. In the last letter, they said, "You are really interested in our tales. We too have started getting interested in them. If you like, we'll send you some more texts." Isn't that brilliant?

The economy—it's not pennies, it's not grains of rice, it's not peanut oil. *Oikos*, it's the house. *Nomia*, it's the rule. It's Greek. *Oikosnomia*, the economy, it's the "rules of the house." Everyone has their rules. The Romans were grocers. The Greeks were tragedians. The Jarai and others are narrators of legends, artists, and musicians. That's their economy. That is how their affairs are settled, judicial disputes and all that, it's brilliant. They sing, they recite, singing verses, "If there is this, there is that—if there is that, there is this, etc., etc." It goes on for hours. It's so beautiful that in the end everyone says okay and the dispute is settled. It's over. No one says any more about it—no prison, no judge, no fine, no debt, nothing. They have a good drink and it's over. Because they do that with their *oikosnomia*, with the rules of their house, through voice, through words, through invention by putting texts end to end, and the winner is the one who speaks best. And that is my economy.

What I'm saying goes a long way. Try to look a bit into the economy of people who don't have an economy in the modern, Western sense of the word. There's a book in that.

Economy of words, too. Let's play on words, as comedians. With three words you can express all sorts of things, because nothing is more condensed than oral literature. You shouldn't think that these are things that are repeated and repeated, lengthened, placed end to end. In three words, you can say many things. One example: a riddle, in four words, four monosyllables: "*Âko' hơoñ tung čum.*" *Âko'*, head—*hơoñ*, caress—*tung*, arse—*čum*, kiss. It's splendid! It's a pipe. Every Jarai kid knows it. In terms of economy of means, [it's very good] eh? Economy of words. You haven't thought about that dimension of the economy. Is it not brilliant?

I learned everything there. I had good teachers at school but never that good. It makes you look again at all the ideas you had before. Four monosyllables that play on words, of course, because it's meant to be shocking. What humor, what economy, four monosyllables! There's a whole philosophy in that. It means "kissing, caressing, playing sex, it's not serious—a good puff is worth more." That's there too. No, I had never learned such fine things before.

[Pause]

JD – I'm working on architecture. Think about construction, in terms of economy of means, it's not garbage. A few bits of bamboo, a few bits of wood and you make a house that can withstand every storm. And that I've seen in the villages. Houses on stilts. Next to that, the Vietnamese have huts made of rammed earth built on the ground. One typhoon and the Vietnamese . . . there's nothing left!

AH – And is the forest also the economy?

JD – Well, here too, I will have a great deal to say, a very great deal to say, because I've fought with the botanists, pedologists, geologists, all the "-ologists" you want.

The technology of swidden agriculture implies a low density of population to the square kilometer. So it's a great luxury that one can only offer oneself in areas where there's no one living. What does it entail? You mark out a perimeter of forest, cut back the undergrowth, cut down the big trees which fall crushing everything that you've already half cut before, then clean up. You set light to it, with firebreaks all around (I've seen this, I've participated!). The flames don't go a meter beyond the firebreaks. Perfect firebreaks. You set light to it. That's the month of April, at the end of the dry season. Because in May, it starts raining a bit. On the ashes, you put the seed in with a dibble stick. Rice, corn, squash, all mixed up. On that—in late May, June, July, August, September even—it rains. You just have to do a little weeding. October is the end of the rains, more or less. In November you harvest, you harvest, you harvest, enough to eat for nearly a year. Really good rice, not that garbage you've been eating in Hanoi. Swidden rice is the best possible. You know that rice is normally an aquatic plant, but that I don't know how many centuries ago, or even millennia, it acclimatized to dry soil that receives a lot of rain. The swidden field is cultivated for two years, maximum three, because after that the soil is exhausted.

I'll give you an example. In the village of Cheo Reo in Jarai country where I was, I built my house on an old swidden field abandoned ten years earlier. There were trees ten centimeters in diameter. One shouldn't say that the practice of swiddening destroys the forest. It grows like weeds. I cut down some of the trees to build my house and replace them with fruit trees. I removed species that weren't useful and put fruit trees in their place—mangoes and things like that. Swiddening does not destroy at all.

So that's the forest economy of those populations. You cut strictly what you need. It's the same thing when you cut a tree as when you build a house. You don't cut ten if you need one. You cut one. When you go hunting, you don't kill ten deer like the French do. They can't even eat it all. It rots. In a pinch you kill one, to feed an entire village for a month. It's economic—and in the old sense of the word. The economy, it's everything, because you have nothing, you're poor. The really economic people are the poor. Real poor people, not the poor people who go to the supermarket and buy things on credit, even cars. Even the kids each have their own car, three or four cars per house. They are fake paupers.

So, next to that, the American economy in Vietnam! For them, the forest, that's where all the Viet Minh are. Defoliant first—very dangerous for people. I had a missionary friend who was badly burned, immobilized for life, just because he received a squirt of it. It was a high-altitude plane. In my garden, twenty kilometers from where the plane passed, I had corn that was curled up like that. Twenty kilometers away! That's the American economy: a good dose of defoliant, then nothing will grow again. On top of that: napalm. I've seen it, I have eyewitness accounts, I even have official UN reports. It will be several centuries before the Indochinese forest starts growing again—if it ever grows again.

The Americans started turning Vietnam into a desert and the Vietnamese continued! When the Americans left like rabbits, they left everything behind, from bulldozers to airplanes. The Vietnamese picked it all up and continued. They drove the bulldozers over what was left of the forest. I saw that too. The gardens of the Moi—not Vietnamese gardens—under the bulldozer. *Vroom*, they pulled everything up! Whenever those good highlanders made swiddens or gardens, they always left a tree here and there [to protect against] erosion, to hold the soil (in these tropical zones, there might be twenty centimeters of cultivable soil). But now, they demolish everything! In ten years, Vietnam will be the Sahara and the highlanders will have nothing more to do but die.

AH – What are the highlanders doing?

JD – Ah, they complain. They can do nothing. They're not recognized by anyone.

AH – I mean economically, to eat.

JD – They farm small gardens.

AH – They can no longer farm swiddens?

JD – There's nothing left to burn: what wasn't burned has been razed by bulldozers. Because for the Vietnamese (as for the Russians, they nicked that from the Russians), the economy means immediate yields.

That's how they killed the Aral Sea and I saw the same trick in Vietnam, twenty kilometers downstream from the village where I was, on the great Apa River. There were geologists, Dutch people, lots of people—this was between 1954 and 1975—who came to study problems, to put in fields of cotton. They found a spot beside the river to grow the cotton. Funny thing, there was no Jarai settlement there.

Against all my advice, against the advice of the Jarai friends and experts, the government decided to put in a huge field of cotton. Vietnamese were settled there, lots of houses, fields. A few months later, the river flooded. The Jarai knew about that. That's why they had never made even a garden there. The cotton, the houses, the Vietnamese, everything headed off towards the sea. There you are: liquidated. That is a Russian way of working, it's a Vietnamese way of working, it's a global way of working. It's what they call economics!

Meanwhile I had the nerve to support the savages' economics, which protects nature. They don't destroy nature. They only destroy to live, just like the tiger (nothing is more cunning than the tiger): if it needs prey, it eats one, not ten. It destroys what it needs, not more. And what's more—and this really beats everything!—when a Jarai cuts down a tree, he says sorry to it first! There, that's where I am. You prune a rose bush, and you say sorry to the rose bush for cutting a branch. I'm afraid to do harm. That is savage. That is economic.

AH – Are there highlanders, people in Laos, China, Burma, who still do swidden farming?

JD – It's difficult to reply. I've been cut off from all information for too many years.

Laos has now become a Vietnamese colony because the Vietnamese see themselves as the heirs of French Indochina. You know, in the 1960s I saw exercise books in Vietnamese schools (in the region governed by Saigon, not by Hanoi). In those exercise books, there was a map of Vietnam that showed Vietnam, Laos, and Cambodia in the same color!

When the French went and settled in Laos and Cambodia, they took Vietnamese with them. It was the French who brought the first Vietnamese to Laos, the first Vietnamese to the high plateaus. Because it was unthinkable for a Frenchman to have a chauffeur or a cook who was a savage with bare feet. He needed a Vietnamese, properly civilized, properly cultivated.

Now the Vietnamese have eaten Laos up completely. They were on the point of eating up Cambodia when the Pol Pot affair happened. [Then came] the Vietnamese military conquest and the Heng Samrin collaborationist regime. Now there's Norodom Sihanouk, the great comedian, who is trying to get back onto the stage. I can't tell you what is happening in Laos or Vietnam. Other than, well, swiddening is forbidden and the bulldozer is permitted. That's economics!

As for the really economic people, the autochthonous people... There's another thing—"autochthonous," which means people who are of the land. The land is theirs. They respect it. There is no written document that says it's theirs but it has been theirs for millennia. They know that and they give the land grace. They nourish it, they respect it. These people's policy is to respect their land. And the policy of those other people—the world economists—is to seize it from them. There are no documents, no texts. The land belongs to no one. And so the government, the authority of the day, wants to do something with it—in particular, the Vietnamese, who are arriving on the high plateaus. It's not their land, they don't give a damn and destroy everything, break everything. They cut everything, bungle everything, for a year or two, to grow vegetables, cabbages, etc.— they need their yields—and abandon everything after a few years. It's true. I've seen it.

For the French [settlers], it was the other way round: Vietnam, Indochina—it was their land. By right of conquest or whatever you like, but it was theirs. They respected the land. They destroyed nothing. The French and the Americans were total opposites. The French made it their land. Many of the settlers and planters were peasants! They knew what land was, and that with land, you respect it, you don't destroy it. For the Americans, there is no land, there is no people, there is nothing. They had to sweep everything away, to make a no man's land between the Philippines and China for their support bases in Southeast Asia. For the French, it was sacred. I've met many of those settlers. I've come across some impossible characters, small settlers [who shamelessly abused] the highlanders, coolies, and all! But it was their land . . .

AH – They invested themselves in it.

JD – Took root! Took root! A civil servant stayed for two years, three years maximum. The settler stayed his whole life, with a return to France every ten years at the very most. That shows their respect for the land. The autochthonous people, the natives, the aboriginals—it's their land, they respect it. But for the Vietnamese settlers today, those who invade all these zones, [it's another story] . . . In the Dran valley, where three or four thousand highlanders lived, from one day to the next there were three hundred thousand Vietnamese. Yes! I have the figures, I have everything, I have documents. It wasn't their land, they destroyed everything. Yields, yields, yields! And now the land is exhausted, there's nothing left, they are dying of hunger. Too much of a hurry. The real peasant isn't in a hurry. You don't pull on a plant to get it to grow—you wait. It's as simple as saying hello. What's more, the Vietnamese have a hatred for trees. The Vietnamese are market gardeners—rice growers and market gardeners: sweep it all away, all clean, all clear.

AH – Are there no trees in the deltas?

JD – Nowhere! Nowhere, in Vietnamese country. They cannot stand a tree. If there is one, they cut it down. Because the land has to yield as much as possible, they do all they can for it to become like a rice field. They've done it so well that ninety million Vietnamese are dying of hunger. And that explains the boat people: they try to get away, because they can no longer stand dying of hunger. There's no political reason, none. Because they don't give a desperate damn for Marxism—I'm talking about the people in Hanoi. They used it to get Russian aid, materiel, to get slogans, political guff, etc., but it was nationalism, patriotism, and whatever you like, exploited.

I know that not everyone can live from the swiddening system. It's a luxury system, for a density from eight or nine to the square kilometer. With high densities, it's not possible. [But] between luxury swiddening and desertification, there may be a solution.

[Pause – The conversation continued the following morning.]

JD – Did you dream last night?

AH – I'm not aware of having done so.

JD – Everyone dreams, even dogs. For a long time, I have got into the habit of using the technique of memorizing dreams as I dream them. And the most interesting ones, I note down. I have ten notebooks or so, because I've had some very interesting ones. It's important for getting to know yourself.

Dreams—I studied them over there with the highlanders. They sometimes had dreams that worried them, and to get rid of them, they had to tell them to someone. Especially among the Jarai, I had women who came to tell me their dreams in the morning. No ethnologist ever had such luck! They told me their dreams. Just like that, it got rid of them. There were no bad effects and I collected the lot. Theoretically for them, I was stronger, I could collect it all and then they were free. There's a lot in that.

AH – What are those dreams like?

JD – You should never interpret them. You have to take them as they are. It's like a piece of music. You shouldn't say it means this or that. You listen, it produces a certain effect, and that's all. You should never interpret them like a painting. You receive, that's it.

Dreams are always extremely short. I have books of dream narratives, people who write a page for a short story that lasted a quarter of a second. To memorize it, you have to take a key word or key image, or a color or something else that you catch. You can express it in three lines . . . More than half of our brain's capacity functions in the state of dreaming. While awake, we use very little of our capacity. People who imagine themselves of little talent, no imagination, banal, when they get down to paying attention to their dreams realize that they possess fantastic riches, an overflowing imagination. Often it's the culture of their family environment or something else that blocks them.

It's the same for language. You know that little children all around the world, babies, are able to pronounce everything that is pronounceable in the world. There's a particular case I've studied: it's the glottal—glottalized consonants /'bo/, /'be/, /'de/. That's why they say "'bonjour" and not "bonjour." The imploded b: "'bon," "'bonjour." And I have heard little French children, babies around two years old, making splendid glottal sounds. Education, the fact of hearing their parents' language, it limits, it limits, it limits, more and more, the means of expression they use to get themselves understood. They used to have enormous capacities. Education puts them on rails. Not much is left.

What I'm telling you about language is like what I was telling you about dreams. They have a point in common: it's the brain. The brain— that controls language. At birth, the brain is capable of all sorts of things. Even before. That's why it's very important that a pregnant woman hears beautiful things, even music. Yes, very important for the child in the mother's belly. There are mothers who do that very well. They speak and it stays. There are memories of what happened before leaving the belly. It exists—memory of the fetal state.

AH – Do the highlanders tell one another their dreams?

JD – One another? In daily life, no. Usually not. [Or when they do] it's to one person only and to get rid of them, as I told you. But in mythology, in oral literature, yes. There's the hero, who is a young man and has a mate, who says he saw a beautiful young woman in a dream, that he held her breasts, etc., etc. Then the others say, "Take us to meet your beauty!" etc. That's the sort of thing that can happen in literature. The dream is told to drive the story.

AH – Literary technique rather than anything else?

JD – Yes, but you can't distinguish the literary from the everyday any more than you can distinguish the sacred from the profane. For them, everything has a sacred character and everything has a literary character. They are literary folk, those peasants, those savages . . . they are literary folk! In ordinary conversation, they slip in assonances, alliterations, rhymes. They can't stop themselves. They are masters of words. It's extraordinary. I have thousands of pages of recorded and transcribed texts, not all of them translated yet. It's crazy. And everyone loves it, young people as well as old. So it's very simple—at school they're no good at maths and very good at literature. The opposite of the Vietnamese, who are maths types—engineers, industrialists—and who aren't much good at literature and philosophy. They don't have any literature, the Vietnamese, almost nothing of any interest. They're quite the opposite.

AH – And among the Jarai, how are the tales narrated?

JD – It depends on the [narrator's] age. Youngsters who are starting to practice narrate anything, anytime, anyhow, to anyone. It's easy for the foreigner who's just arrived, who knows a little of the language and starts with the kids. You learn a great deal, already. You know there's a story, there's a guy who has a hero's name, etc. And then, after a few years when you are coping with the language better, you manage to find someone who narrates it to you in four or five hours continuously. Because with the kid, it lasts ten minutes. It's like "Cinderella" or "Little Red Hiding Hood." You ask a kid to tell it, it lasts three minutes. If there are still old storytellers in France, they'll take hours telling it.

The circumstances are not the same at all. For the child, there are no circumstances. For the storyteller, there are times of the year: times when there's no work in the rice fields and when it's raining. Then, if they feel like it—it's out of the question to ask them—in the evening, at night, in their house, in the house of a neighbor or friends where they're spending the evening, they'll tell a story. It can last an hour, it can last five hours, until dawn . . . And you have that throughout Southeast Asia. The rest of the world I haven't studied.

There is no particular rite. There's just a time of the year, an hour of the day [when there's less work and you can stay up a bit late] . . . Because you know, when you work in the rice fields, you go to bed at half past seven. When you do nothing all day because it's been raining too hard, or simply because the rice has just been harvested and there's nothing to do—that's the best time, mid-December to the end of January. Then they have nothing to do. House repairs, they do that from February. Preparing the fields is done in March–April. So at that time, at the end of the year, December–January, it's easier to hear tales. It's spontaneous. They are really chaotic. If they want to, they tell stories, that's all.

AH – There aren't any professional storytellers?

JD – No, no professionals. It's not like in Africa with the griot. They aren't paid. They do it for pleasure. They don't drink, never before storytelling—it damages the voice. They drink afterwards. And, you know, they're not very sober—when they drink, they drink too much and then they can't tell stories. They know it very well.

AH – And they only use their voice . . . ?

JD – There's no music. Many of them are musicians, too—everyone is a musician. Almost everyone has a musical instrument they've made themselves. Those they make are wind and string instruments—flutes, whistles, and types of zithers. Almost everyone plays an instrument but there is never any accompaniment with the tale. There are no gestures. They're sitting down.

AH – Many people?

JD – Oh no, ten or so people in the hut. You don't organize an assembly for that, given that it's unpredictable. You don't know that he's going to tell a story. I had friends there, in the village, who said, "So and so is a storyteller. He's coming to spend the evening in our house. He might tell a story, I don't know." Some came and told stories in my house, because they knew I'd enjoy it, on their own.

AH – Can you give me an example of a tale?

JD – Many. I learned to be a storyteller . . .

At Cerisy. I don't know if you know the conferences at Cerisy. It's a chateau in Normandy where there's a cultural center, and every summer there are ten or so conferences on specific subjects. I was invited—seven or eight years ago at least—to a conference on myths and mythology. I gave a lecture and asked for the chance to tell a story in the evening in the great hall of the chateau. So they prepared the chateau's loft—a real cathedral, splendid! There were about fifty people. I asked them to serve drinks. They served punch, things like that. I started to tell a story. I told a whole lot of stories. It started around ten in the evening or so, just after dinner. At midnight they were exhausted but still asked for more. And from memory! I had no text, I hadn't brought anything with me. I hadn't thought I'd tell stories at all. I thought I'd give my lecture—I had the lecture in my head—and that's all. And when I said to myself, "But maybe they'd like me to tell a story," I went walking in the chateau's gardens all day before that evening, to rememorize—without any notes, nothing—to rememorize those fine stories. Then *hop!* I was off!

Barefoot in the Mud:
Reflections on Jacques Dournes

Oscar Salemink

Jacques Dournes was a man with many faces. He was a marvelous maverick, an irreverent reverend, a missionary celebrating pagan culture, an ethnographer despising professional anthropologists, a self-styled "fieldworker" in the literal sense of the term—with his feet in the mud—who managed to write at least eighteen book-length publications, a celibate man who admired and enjoyed the eroticism of Jarai culture. He was not an easy man, and he got easily and often into trouble because of his idiosyncratic thoughts and behavior. As Andrew Hardy's interview with him shows, Dournes was sarcastic, provocative, sometimes cynical, often comical. He was a man of big thoughts that had to go against the grain—or else it was no fun to entertain such thoughts in the first place. The question whether a statement that he made was true or not mattered little to him, as long as it expressed his unique views—unique in the sense that the statement was based on his unique life experience. After all, no other person had his unique experience, which seemed sufficient reason to reject or even despise the views offered by the rest of mankind.

We could speculate whether he had always been that way, but it is clear that he was an adventurer and lone wolf who loathed formal institutions. Ordained as a priest in 1945, he came to Vietnam in 1946 as an apprentice missionary, in the wake of the French military attempt to regain control of their former colony, which had been wrested from their hands first by the Japanese, and then by Vietnamese nationalists led by Ho Chi Minh. From the moment he set foot on Vietnamese soil, and more in particular the Central Highlands, he came to a place he could call home. This was a place without too many formal, bureaucratic institutions that hampered his sense of adventure, yet under the umbrella of one of the strongest institutions in the region, namely the Catholic Church. Being deployed in Djiring district [now Di Linh] in the province now known as Lâm Đồng, he met the indigenous population of the Central Highlands who would capture his heart forever. Having escaped the dreariness of postwar France, he had arrived at a place where he felt he belonged, finally. He was enamored by the highlanders' lifestyles—in his view, simple yet beautiful, meaningful, authentic, and honest, so different from those of the French, either in France or in Indochina. He also found the highlanders' lifestyles vastly different from those of the ethnic Vietnamese with their nationalist movement that he was sent to fight, institutionally speaking, as a French Catholic priest.

He took some parts of his job seriously and other parts less so. He was not very serious about missionizing in the sense of converting the local population to Christianity, because converting them would mean destroying the very culture that he loved so much. He was serious about studying the highland societies of the Koho, Sre, Mạ, and especially Jarai (among whom he lived from 1955–70) — their cultures, languages, environments—recording their stories and poetry, their botanical and zoological knowledge, their "legal" procedures of reconciliation. He was suspicious of the changes brought about by war, by modernity, by the French, the ethnic Vietnamese, and later the Americans, which he interpreted in terms of cultural destruction, producing a generation of *jeunesse déracinée* [deracinated youth], who went into the army and adopted modern ways:

> At present an alarming number of youngsters are recruited as mercenaries in this foreign war, which interests them only as a convenient life style.[1]

---

1. Dournes, *Coordonnés*, 262.

In other words, while deploring the changes wrought by colonization and war, Dournes turned out to be a cultural conservationist who appreciated local culture only on his own terms, that is, if it would not change.

Dournes became so enamored with these people and their cultural practices that he thought he could become one of them. He published his first major ethnographic publication under the *nom de plume* Dam Bo, which was the name given to him by the Koho and Sre group, trying to convince his audience of his integration into montagnard society. Writing in hindsight, Dournes (1977) would analyze this pose of himself (Dam Bo) and Georges Condominas (Yo Sar Luk) and Jean Boulbet (Dam Böt), in romantic terms:

> Yo Sar Luk [Georges Condominas], Dam Böt [Jean Boulbet] . . . and myself, Dam Bo at the time, publicized our "savage" names as the program of our dreams. This was integration into a people, quite different from our community of origin, knowing well that we remained the Whites in the eyes of those who, we pretended, had adopted us—although we had been imposed upon them—and for whom our strangeness excused our marginal lives and our privileges, within a context of colonization.[2]

In this passage Dournes displayed a retrospective awareness that this "nativist" claim to ethnographic authority was rather ludicrous. In the eyes of the highland groups that they studied, "Condo," Boulbet, and Dournes himself may have seemed unusual colonizers but nevertheless represented colonial power and privilege. What he fails to note, however, is that his desire to immerse himself into highlander culture and to belong to the local community stands in stark contrast with his own life trajectory of abandoning his homeland, cutting ties with his family and native community. This desire to belong was predicated on the distance that he created from his own lifeworld. Moreover, he could only cherish an illusion of "cultural belonging" because he was so different and therefore was accepted on his own terms rather than as a full-fledged community member, with all the responsibilities and obligations that entails. He thus

2. Dournes, *PUT*, 76.

hypocritically denied to young highlanders the cultural right to chart their own trajectory—something he took for granted in his own life. Dournes was expelled twice from Vietnam. The first time, in 1954, he was removed on the orders of Bảo Đại, the emperor under French tutelage who, after accepting direct French rule in the Central Highlands, enjoyed the right to call the highlands his personal "crown domain." Bảo Đại's own eviction from Vietnam by South Vietnam's first president Ngô Đình Diệm allowed Dournes to return to the highlands, where he was assigned to a place where the local populations seemed invulnerable to missionary conversion efforts: the Jarai heartland of Cheo Reo (later known as Phú Bổn and Ayun Pa). He subsequently fell completely in love with Jarai culture—or better, his version of it. As a missionary, he is reputed for not having converted one single Jarai person to Catholicism, because he hesitated to try and change a culture that he considered to be closer to the original Christian ideal than the Western culture from which he came.

After his second banishment from Vietnam in 1970, where he quickly found—indeed earned—asylum within the French academic system, his banishment from the place he called home made him suffer greatly. As happens with people in diaspora, he identified more and more with the place and people he had lost but—given the physical distance—not with the place and people themselves, but with those in his memory and in his imagination. Losing the physical connection with the missionary and ethnographic "field"—no longer *pieds nus dans la boue* [barefoot in the mud] as he phrased it—he converted to a religiously held vision of Jarai culture that no longer existed. In France he tried to become Jarai—more Jarai than the Jarai themselves, who were already converting in droves to evangelical Christianity during his lifetime, thus abandoning many of their cultural and religious practices.

It was in this period between 1970 and his retirement in 1987—and particularly between 1972 and 1978—that he worked in a delirious frenzy, putting out one book after another, on the Koho and Sre in Djiring/Di Linh but more so on "his" proud and joyous Jarai, over time changing his version and his classification of Jarai culture. Ultimately, his ethnographic *oeuvre* would culminate in his lyrical and simultaneously vitriolic *Pötao:*

une théorie du pouvoir chez les Indochinois Jörai (1977). This book and his lyrical *Forêt femme folie, une traversée de l'imaginaire Jörai* (1978) were published during an extremely productive writing spell which saw him publish five full monographs in the scope of just three years. In doing so he erected an amazing memorial of and tribute to Jarai life as it had once been, before it was changed forever by the combined outside forces of French colonialism, of American imperialist belligerence, of Vietnamese nationalism and communism, of global and local markets and forms of neoliberal governance, along with the inside forces of desire for modernity, as expressed in Jarai participation in communist and/or autonomy movements and in Jarai conversion to Protestantism. Dournes was well aware of all these developments, as expressed in a variety of ethnohistorical overview analyses (1975, 1978b, 1980).

As noted above, his *Forêt femme folie* constitutes a lyrical tribute to the ways of thinking, of living, and of loving among the Jarai, described from an insider's perspective. Without doubt, however, Dournes's *chef d'oeuvre* remains his *Pötao: une théorie du pouvoir chez les Indochinois Jörai* (1977), which seeks to detail a political system without political institutions, without state, without military, without politico-religious doctrine. His pen dipped in vitriol, he ridicules outsiders—all outsiders—who misunderstood the Jarai and the Potao: lowland courts, colonial administrators (like Léopold Sabatier), missionaries, ethnographers. There is only one person who truly understands the complexity of Jarai thought and of the Jarai lifeworld, as expressed in the ritual-political system of the Potao, and that is Dournes himself—and the Jarai themselves, of course, to whom this book is a marvelous tribute, a great attempt at understanding, describing, and analyzing their lifeworld.

After Dournes's retirement and retreat from noisy Paris—where he lived in the rue Broca, named after one of France's first anthropologists—to the Gard in 1987, his productivity waned. It was not just his fragile health but also his bitterness that did him in. He was bitter at his removal from Vietnam, from his home in the Central Highlands. He was bitter at the changes in the highlands, which would make the Jarai lifeworld as he knew it (and perhaps imagined it) disappear forever. He was bitter at the perceived lack of recognition for his scholarly work born out of the mud—in stark contrast with the academic mandarins ruling the Paris-based scholarly elite. This bitterness gave rise to sarcastic comments by colleagues among that elite, recorded in this book by Andrew Hardy, about his particular "point of view"—comments which were justified in the sense that, scientifically speaking, we are not required to agree with all his opinions. But it was this same bitterness that proved fertile ground for his splendid œuvre—perhaps more fertile even than the mud in which he liked to stomp, whether or not he was barefoot.

French Transcript of the Interview with Jacques Dournes

(Bagard, France, February 1–2, 1992)

AH – Heureusement que je ne vous ai pas amené du vin !

JD – Quelle horreur !

AH – Je me suis dis...

JD – ... « C'est un Français, donc il doit boire du vin ». Ben non ! Alors, qu'est-ce que vous voulez savoir ?

AH – Je cherche un sujet pour une thèse.

JD – Maintenant on ne fait plus de thèses d'état, on fait des thèses d'université ! Ce n'est pas difficile de faire une thèse. Vous soutenez n'importe quelle connerie devant un jury qui n'y connaît rien du tout, vous êtes le seul à connaître la question et hop ! Vous partez avec la mention très bien. Pas compliqué. Il suffit d'avoir un directeur de thèse qui est de connivence et c'est tout. Pas compliqué une thèse.

Mais une thèse d'état en Sorbonne, avec Lévi-Strauss au jury, moi je peux m'en vanter. Oui ! J'étais tellement sûr de mon coup. Il y avait une foule dans l'amphithéâtre de la Sorbonne, c'était bourré. Je me suis bien marré. De tous les membres du jury [Lévi-Strauss] est le seul qui a lu ma thèse et c'est le seul avec lequel j'ai discuté. Il m'attaquait sur des problèmes d'analyse structurale. Il m'attaquait, je lui répondais, c'était du ping-pong. C'était brillant de tous les côtés, magnifique. C'était le 23 juin 1973. Ça fait presque vingt ans. J'étais déjà vieux, hein ? Cinquante ans. À l'époque, les thèses d'état en Sorbonne, il y en a peu qui avaient moins de cinquante ans. J'ai soutenu ma thèse un an après Condominas, un an après Haudricourt et tant d'autres. Donc j'étais un des plus jeunes à cinquante ans à soutenir une thèse d'état. C'était sérieux à ce moment là une thèse d'état, ah oui.

AH – Et la thèse de Gourou, *Les paysans du delta*, c'était une thèse d'état ?

JD – Gourou était un grand bonhomme, un homme droit, parfaitement droit. Le truc ce n'est pas mal, c'est lisible. C'est l'ouvrage qui fait référence actuellement. Je ne suis pas géographe. Je ne connais pas le Tonkin, ce qu'on appelait le Tonkin en ces temps-là, ce qu'on appelait ensuite le Nord Vietnam. Mais il me semble difficile quand-même de parler des paysans du delta en s'en tenant à l'[agri]culture. Il y a l'homme, ce qu'il fait dans sa maison, sa langue. Gourou, il ne parlait pas vietnamien.

AH – Ah oui dis donc.

JD – Oh quelques mots, « nyang nyang nyong ong ong », n'importe quoi. Comme Delvert pour le Cambodge ; Delvert ne sait pas un mot de cambodgien. Il ne sait pas ce que c'est que de tremper les pieds nus dans la rizière.

Moi j'en suis là. Si on n'a pas été pieds nus dans la rizière on ne sait rien, parce que tout se passe dans la tête des gens. L'économique, l'agronomique, ce sont des épiphénomènes et ce n'est pas ça qui explique les phénomènes. Que ce soit Gourou pour le Tonkin, que ce soit Delvert pour le Cambodge, que ce soit beaucoup d'autres, ils n'ont pas trempé dans la boue. Ce sont des sociologues, il y a des chiffres, il y a des rendements à l'hectare, il y a des trucs comme ça. Pour moi, ça n'a aucun intérêt. Pour moi, hein ! Je ne dis pas que pour les économistes ça n'en ait pas.

L'intérêt pour moi, c'est l'homme vis-à-vis de son milieu, qu'est-ce qu'il va en faire, qu'est-ce qu'il va en sortir, en diachronie, en suivant le fil des siècles et l'évolution des politiques et de la psychologie des hommes. Comment l'homme, pieds nus dans sa rizière avec de la boue jusqu'à mi-jambes, réfléchit, réagit, pense et rêve à autre chose aussi. C'est ça qui est intéressant. Le rendement à l'hectare je m'en fous, je n'ai jamais mesuré ça. Je suis anthropologue, je ne suis pas géographe.

[*Discussion sur le problème du choix d'un sujet de thèse.*]

JD – Alors là vous me parliez de dates. Vous me parliez de 1950 à 1960.

AH – Oui.

JD – Ça n'existe pas. Si vous voulez prendre une tranche...

AH – 1945 à 1954.

JD – Voilà ! Bon, vous avez trouvé tout seul, ce n'est pas la peine que je m'époumone. 1946 : la reconquête gaulliste de l'Indochine. 1954 : la défaite française. Ça, c'est un bon morceau.

Vous savez très bien que les dates historiques ne sont pas les dates de siècle. Le XXe siècle a commencé en 1919, le XXIe siècle a commencé en 1991, hein ? Ce sont les événements humains qui fabriquent les époques, les dates et les séquences. Alors pour l'Indochine, un petit travail historique et que personne n'ose franchement aborder : 1946-1954.

AH – Oui, la guerre d'Indochine.

JD – Je connais à fond. J'ai débarqué en Indochine en 1946 et j'étais foutu à la porte en 1954 ! Je connais à fond, de tous les côtés : côté français, côté vietnamien, côté des minorités.

AH – J'hésite aussi bien de reprendre ce sujet-là : la guerre, la guerre...

JD – Ce n'est pas une guerre ! Mais non !

AH – La haine, alors, la haine.

JD – Non plus ! C'est du temps des Américains qu'il y eut la guerre. Je parle du temps des Français. J'ai connu des amiraux, des généraux, des chefs des provinces, des administrateurs. J'ai discuté avec tout ce monde-là et je me suis fait ma petite raison là-dessus. Et je vous garantis que, de 1946 à 1954, on ne faisait pas la guerre. Elle a commencé en 1954.

AH – On faisait quoi ?

JD – Bon, c'était... c'était la comédie. La comédie ! On trichait, de tous les côtés. Les Français voulaient faire du fric. Il faut connaître aussi toute l'histoire qui s'est passée juste avant 1946. Que de 1940 à 1945, l'Indochine française était sous la coupe de l'amiral Decoux. Pétiniste à bloc, hein ! Et les chefs de province, les évêques, tous les Français [*JD chante :*] « Maréchal, nous voilà ! Devant toi, le sauveur de la France. »

Alors donc voilà une Indochine ex-française, devenue pétiniste pro-allemande. Donc pas hostile aux Japonais. En 1945, coup de force japonais en Indochine. Là, Decoux et compagnie ont été complètement cocufiés par les Japonais. Les Japs prennent le pouvoir, les Français en camps de concentration et les Japs ont cette idée géniale de donner leur indépendance aux Vietnamiens ! L'indépendance du Vietnam vient de la grâce du Mikado. C'est historiquement vrai !

[Puis] De Gaulle décide en 1946 la reconquête militaire de l'Indochine. Alors, au printemps-été 1946, il y a quelques bateaux chargés de militaires qui quittent Marseille pour aller à Saigon, pour la reconquête. Moi, j'ai fait parti du premier bateau civil, en septembre-octobre 1946, donc je suis absolument contemporain aux événements.

À ce moment-là, Ho Chi Minh, qui n'était pas une canaille, a dit, [en] décembre 1946, « Que les Français nous envoient des instituteurs mais pas des militaires ! ». Je l'ai entendu. Moi, petit jeune – j'avais 24 ans – je déclare en pleine assemblée de tous ces curés, évêques, administrateurs et tout ça : « Ho Chi Minh a raison, la culture française mais pas la bataille ». Oh, je me suis fait bien voir dès le début, oi oi oi ! Ho Chi Minh n'en a jamais rien su, mais moi j'en ai reçu plein les gencives. Il avait raison : il se trouve qu'aujourd'hui, il n'y a pas un Vietnamien qui parle français au Vietnam.

Et alors il se trouve que par-dessus le marché, ce De Gaulle de mon cul, nomme comme gouverneur général Thierry d'Argenlieu – religieux Carmes déchaussé (il a toujours gardé ses godasses, le déchaussé !) – qu'on appelait aussi Ruolz, parce que Ruolz c'est une marque de produit de fourchettes [qui] tient lieu d'argenterie. C'était la risée de tout le monde, Thierry d'Argenlieu.

AH – D'Argenlieu a renvoyé en France beaucoup de Pétinistes d'Indochine ?

JD – Quasi tous. Et pire que ça. Il y avait l'évêque, le dernier Français évêque de Saigon. Je ne sais pas si vous étiez au courant, à l'époque, de la Légion pétiniste ?

AH – Non.

JD – Il faut connaître cette histoire-là ! Vous ne pouvez pas parler de l'Indochine sans connaître l'histoire de la France à la même époque, c'est impossible. Non, on ne peut pas couper une tranche dans le gâteau sans connaître le reste, parce que l'histoire humaine c'est terriblement imbriqué, hein ?

Bon. Pétain organisait la Légion qui est devenue la Milice par la suite. Des gens dévoués, une troupe dévouée à lui, troupe civile, militaire, tous des gens complètement dévoués. Donc l'évêque de Saigon était chef de la Légion en Indochine, chef de tous les Français pétinistes, « Maréchal nous voilà tac tac tac ».

Bon, là je passe, coupez ! coupez !

[Pause]

J'ai de la voix ! Elle est unique ma voix. Je suis comédien ! Et la comédie, ce n'est pas le mensonge, c'est la plus grande vérité qui existe. Je ne mens jamais. Je mets en scène des trucs à comprendre. Je suis comédien dans la peau. C'est le plus beau des métiers. À condition de le savoir, parce que tout le monde est comédien, tout le monde joue une pseudo-comédie ; les comédiens sont les seuls à savoir que eux jouent la comédie. Ils se dominent, ils ont quelque chose à dire. C'est très fort ce que je vous dis.

AH – Ils ne se prennent pas pour des sérieux ?

JD – Je me prends tellement peu au sérieux que je suis incapable de prendre qui que ce soit au sérieux, ha ha !

Alors continuons sur le Vietnam. Je vais vous donner une généralité sur la vie économique. C'est que pendant tout la période française [la période] des méchants colonialistes, c'est-à-dire celle que j'ai connue de 1946 à 1954, tout le monde mangeait bien. Les routes étaient circulables ; le train de Saigon à Hanoi ça roulait et les gens bouffaient bien. Oh, il y avait les escarmouches en brousse, le Viet Minh contre les Français, contre je ne sais pas quoi. C'était des escarmouches, ce n'était rien de plus.

Le Vietnam, c'est un pays franchement riche. Je n'ai jamais vu quelqu'un avoir faim, même sous la guerre américaine. Sauf dans les camps de concentration – parce que les Américains avaient fait des camps de concentration pas seulement pour les Vietnamiens, les soi-disant communistes, mais pour les minorités ethniques, pour les montagnards, les moïs – là-dedans on crevait de faim copieusement. Mais dans les villages, j'avais une quarantaine de villages dans un rayon de dix kilomètres autour de chez moi, une vallée très riche, je n'ai jamais vu quelqu'un avoir faim, mais jamais !

Le Vietnam exportait du riz, oui, et depuis l'époque américaine le Vietnam a importé du riz de Thaïlande. Ça en dit long et pourquoi ? Parce que l'empire stalinien de Hanoi réquisitionnait tout le riz pour l'envoyer en Russie, parce que les Russes avaient aidé les Vietnamiens à prendre leur indépendance. Dette de guerre. Parce que surtout sous l'époque américaine, les chars, les quelques chars vietnamiens, les quelques avions vietnamiens, tout l'armement était entièrement russe. Et ce qui est marrant c'est que ça transitait par la Chine qui détestait les Russes. On fermait les yeux, on fermait les yeux, tout transitait par la Chine et puis ça arrivait au Vietnam. Alors dette de guerre : sous la période jusqu'à Gorbatchev, les Vietnamiens envoyaient tout leur riz en Russie. Résultat, plus de riz pour les paysans vietnamiens.

À partir du départ des Français, mais surtout après 1975, c'est à partir de 1975 que c'était la catastrophe pour le Vietnam. C'est là qu'il y a eu les boat people. Le régime de Hanoi a fait la réunification du Vietnam, ce qui n'était pas une évidence historique. Tandis que la Corée – il n'y a jamais eu deux Corées dans l'histoire – c'est un problème uniquement politique et américain celui de la Corée, comme de l'Allemagne. Tandis que le Vietnam a toujours eu le royaume du Nord [et] le royaume du Sud. Ils ne se sont jamais aimés. Ils ont des dialectes tels que quelqu'un de Hanoi et quelqu'un de Saigon ont du mal à se comprendre, sans parler des gens de Huê qui parlent encore un autre dialecte, façon de mettre les accents, les tons. Ils se comprennent tout juste. Au téléphone ils ne se comprennent pas du tout. Il faut écrire pour se comprendre !

À partir de 1975, le régime de Hanoi imposait ses structures, notamment économiques. Il n'y avait plus de propriété privée. Tous les travailleurs donnaient tout à l'État. L'État leur donnait trois conneries pour 300 tonnes. C'est ce qui s'est passé en Russie, qui est un pays extrêmement riche. Ça regorge de tout la Russie. C'est une stupidité d'envoyer de l'aide alimentaire actuellement tant qu'elle n'est pas distribuée, pour la bonne raison qu'il n'y a pas de réseau de distribution. Il faut demander à tel bureau, qui va demander à tel bureau, qui va demander à tel bureau, puis entre deux il y a un flémard qui oublie de téléphoner, puis ça reste des mois comme ça, des patates en train de pourrir, dépassées de date et cetera. C'est ça, le régime.

Dégoûtés de ne plus avoir de propriété privée, dégoûtés de devoir tout donner à l'État, les paysans vietnamiens – et aussi montagnards – ont produit de moins en moins. Résultat, ils n'ont rien à bouffer. Les riches importent du riz de Thaïlande alors que c'était l'inverse quand j'étais au Vietnam.

[Pause]

AH – Est-ce que la guerre d'Indochine a eu un grand impact sur l'économie ?

JD – Là, il faut nuancer. Parce qu'il faut très bien distinguer la guerre française et la guerre américaine. La guerre française c'était pour défendre une colonie et même une colonie de peuplement, ce que les Américains n'ont jamais fait. Des Français, [des] familles entières, des planteurs s'installaient et restaient des décennies. Ils s'intéressaient au pays. Ils aimaient la terre, ils faisaient souche, quelquefois avec une femme vietnamienne ; ça ne marchait pas si mal. La mère de Marguerite Duras et bien d'autres… On reparlera de *L'Amant*, oui, parce que je déteste ce machin-là.

Ce n'était pas si terrible la colonisation. Oh, il y avait des bagnes, Poulo Condore – quelques dizaines de gars qu'on appelait communistes et qu'on a fourrés au bagne – [mais] il n'y a pas eu de scènes horribles. Sur le plan économique, les Français avaient des plantations – caoutchouc, thé, café – qui ne profitaient qu'aux Européens. Parce que les Vietnamiens ne se servaient pas de ce caoutchouc, les Vietnamiens ne boivent pas de café et leur thé ils en ont tellement. Enfin les plantations étaient uniquement pour le fric des planteurs français.

AH – Et les gens qui travaillaient, les Vietnamiens ?

JD – La plupart : des gens du Nord. Parce que dans le Sud il y a beaucoup de rizières, des rizières très riches de la Cochinchine. Alors ils travaillaient dans la rizière. Il y avait surplus de riz, parce qu'on en vendait partout. J'ai toujours connu le Vietnam comme exporteur [sic] de riz. [Mais] il fallait des coolies sur les plantations. [Et] comme les montagnards – c'est leur caractère, ils sont anarchistes, aargh ! – ils ne veulent pas travailler pour un patron, aaargh ! Bon, inutile avec les montagnards, les moï, hein ? [Donc] on a fait venir des Vietnamiens du Nord ; densité de 80 à 90 au kilomètre carré, ça dépasse la Hollande, ahurissant comme densité. On a fait venir des gens du Nord, ils travaillaient bien.

AH – Ils en ont profité ?

JD – Ils n'étaient pas malheureux. Ils étaient payés, ils étaient nourris, ils avaient des logements, ils n'étaient pas malheureux. Il y avait une espèce de boutique dans la plantation où ils pouvaient acheter – pris sur leur salaire – des vêtements, du tabac, des bricoles. Il n'y a pas l'argent comme il y a au village.

AH – Ils ne pouvaient pas acheter sur le marché ?

JD – Les plantations sont éloignées des centres-villes. C'était en brousse, il n'y avait aucun transport en commun. Une fois [que] le pauvre coolie vietnamien du Nord s'installait là bas il ne bougeait plus. C'était eux le marché !

AH – [Mais] en 1945 après le coup de force, ils ont tous quitté les plantations.

JD – Il n'y en avait pas beaucoup en 1945, des gens du Nord. Non, c'est après 1946 que ça a commencé. Avant c'était des petites entreprises familiales, pas de gros gros machins, sinon Michelin. Mais Michelin, c'était le caoutchouc et c'était limitrophe entre Vietnam et Cambodge. Non, les plus grosses plantations étaient sur le Cambodge, province de Mondolkiri. Les plantations se sont développées entre 1946 et 1954. Développement énorme ! Je l'ai vu de jour en jour, je voyais les progrès. J'ai vu des planteurs français, fusil à la main, aller dans mes villages, obliger mes « moïs » aller partir sur leurs plantations. J'ai porté plainte. L'administrateur français m'a soutenu. Il a été vidé, envoyé en Afrique. Et moi quelques années après, j'ai été vidé. Parce que les planteurs avec la Banque d'Indochine et Bảo Đại, c'est la même chose tout ça ! J'étais appelé « le curé rouge » par Bảo Đại. Il a obligé mon rapatriement.

Bon, ceux qui travaillaient sur les plantations… Les Vietnamiens y allaient volontiers. Puis les gens faisaient souche, ils ont construit leur maison. Ils y sont toujours. C'est eux qui ont les plantations maintenant, avec un apport chinois, il ne faut pas oublier. Bien sûr le patron est chinois. Ce sont les Chinois qui ont remplacé les Français comme patrons des grandes plantations.

AH – C'est toujours les Chinois maintenant ? Après 1978-1979 ?

JD – Je manque d'informations. Mais tant que j'y étais c'était des Chinois qui étaient les gros patrons des Vietnamiens du Nord qui travaillaient, pas malheureux du tout. Tout ça faisait la richesse du Vietnam : thé, café, caoutchouc. Surtout thé et café, le caoutchouc a baissé régulièrement parce qu'on a fait du caoutchouc synthétique tout simplement. Thé et café, ça marchait vraiment bien sur le plan économique.

Puis alors les montagnards… Quand on leur foutait la paix, ils mangeaient bien ! Une densité de 8 au kilomètre carré, pensez ! A Hanoi, 90 au kilomètre carré. Alors sur les hauts plateaux – mon cher pays – c'était du luxe ! On gratte un peu la terre, on met quelques grains de riz, on en a plein plein plein et puis du bon riz. Je l'ai vu. On bouffait vraiment bien, il n'y a aucun problème.

AH – Dans le delta du Sud ?

JD – [Dans le] delta du Sud, on faisait trois récoltes de riz par an. Une terre très très riche les alluvions du Mékong. C'était bourré d'alluvions, ça déboulait, ça déboulait… ça va boucher la mer. Finalement, l'Indochine va rejoindre la Malaisie si ça continue comme ça. Dans deux mille ans, ça sera peut-être le cas.

Il y a deux économies. Il y a l'économie interne, comment les gens vivent. Les paysans vietnamiens comme les paysans montagnards, [des] petites exploitations familiales, [une] terre ultra riche. Je parle d'avant 1954, tant que c'était la soi-disant guerre française. On pouvait aller chez n'importe quel paysan ; j'étais nourri comme ça, je me régalais ! Des petits poissons, des crabes de rizières, un tas de trucs délicieux, du vrai *nước mắm*, ha ha ! [Le] paysan vietnamien [et le] paysan montagnard se ressemblent énormément. Ils n'ont jamais été ennemis, on a inventé des trucs là-dessus. Ennemis héréditaires ! C'est comme les Français et les Allemands, wah ! Ou les Français et les Anglais ; on n'est plus au temps de Jeanne d'Arc. À qui roulerait le plus l'autre, oui oui oui ! Ça marchait très bien. Il n'y avait pas de rixe, il n'y avait pas de bataille, il n'y avait rien. [Voilà pour] l'économie interne. Économie externe : exportation considérable – thé, café, caoutchouc – qui donnaient des devises énormes au Vietnam. Donc tout était très équilibré.

AH – Et les Vietnamiens avaient un rôle important dans cette économie ?

JD – Les Chinois surtout.

AH – Les Vietnamiens, ils étaient…

JD – … des exécuteurs. Jusqu'en 1954, tout le monde vivait bien. Tout le monde avait dans la maison de quoi manger tous les jours et de quoi nourrir dix gosses. Oui, dix gosses c'est une moyenne dans la famille. Là j'ai fait des statistiques chez les Jörai. Moyenne de naissances : dix par mariage. Survivants : sept, au bout de trois ans. Pas mal, hein ? Ce qui fait que les Vietnamiens, qui étaient à peine 40 millions en 1946, soient maintenant 90 millions, beaucoup plus nombreux que les Français sur un territoire beaucoup plus petit. Normal qu'ils envahissent le Laos et le Cambodge. Quand un Américain descendait un Vietnamien dans la guerre, une femme vietnamienne mettait au monde deux gosses. C'était coulé d'avance la politique militaire américaine. Ça pond, ça pond, ça pond et puis tout le monde [travaille]. À quatre ans, le gosse commence à travailler dans le jardin. On cultive les ruisseaux, le bord du chemin, on cultive tout. On met des patates douces, on met du piment, on met des arachides, on met tout, jusqu'au bord de la route. C'est des travailleurs infatigables, increvables les Vietnamiens. Alors là, pour le travail je les respecte. Qu'est-ce qu'ils travaillent !

Il n'y a qu'à voir à Paris, les boat people, ils arrivent dans le 13e arrondissement, sans un sou. Ils commencent par faire la plonge dans un restaurant vietnamien. Ça dure six mois maximum. Après ça ils servent à table. Après ça ils aident à la cuisine. Et en moins d'un an ils ouvrent un restaurant à côté. Ils font fortune. Chapeau pour le travail. Et par-dessus le marché, c'est bon ce qu'ils font. C'est sain, c'est frais, c'est bon, c'est propre. Personne n'a été malade d'un plat vietnamien. Les Vietnamiens se sont imposés. J'ai entendu un commerçant Vietnamien à Paris, Place Maubert, me dire « Ah Paris, c'est notre plus belle colonie ». Ce n'est pas beau ça ? Eux qui colonisent la France à leur tour, avec beaucoup d'humour et beaucoup d'amitié pour la France. Oh, je trouve ça magnifique. Joli retour des choses, sans lutte, sans rien de violent mais en s'imposant par le travail et la qualité.

Alors vous voyez, l'économie familiale interne a très bien fonctionné tant que c'était en anarchie. Parce que les Français ne vérifiaient pas ce qui se passait dans les villages. Hanoi était très loin et n'avait pas encore beaucoup de visées sur le Sud. Donc c'était pratiquement ce qu'on appelait le communisme vietnamien, c'est-à-dire de la commune. Sous ce temps-là, c'était impeccable. Tout le monde en a de très bons souvenirs. Parce que les Français n'ont vraiment pas voulu se battre.

Quand j'étais jeune, j'étais comme mon petit chien, j'étais fureteur, j'allais partout, j'étais dans les camps militaires, dans les campements, dans les petits bastions perdus dans la forêt. Puis je voyais des Français paumés à trois-quatre, avec quelques montagnards autour. Une frousse épouvantable, ils n'osaient pas sortir de leur poste. Ils étaient ravitaillés par hélicoptère, ha ! Ils ne voulaient pas se battre. Ils ne se battaient pas ! Il a fallu quelques généraux absurdes pour vouloir organiser une grande bataille dans le Nord du Vietnam pour reprendre un Vietnam qui leur avait déjà échappé.

AH – Ils voulaient quand même défendre leurs intérêts économiques.

JD – Pas les militaires, ils s'en foutaient. Les militaires et les planteurs ne pouvaient pas se voir. Bah ! Il n'y avait pas de collusion française là-dedans, pas du tout.

AH – Et les industriels, les planteurs, comment ils s'en sortaient ?

JD – Pénards comme tout ! Personne n'allait sur leurs plantations. De temps en temps, il y a eu le Viet Minh qui allait descendre un pauvre coolie pour faire peur. Pas grande chose, jusqu'en 1954. Des bricoles. Non, ce n'était pas vraiment la guerre. Les planteurs français là étaient très contents.

AH – Ils pensaient rester ?

JD – Oui, tout le monde pensait rester. Moi aussi. Bon, eux avaient des ennemis, moi j'en avais d'autres, mais tout le monde pensait rester.

AH – Et les Chinois dans tout ça ?

JD – Oh les Chinois, dans l'intérieur pas grande chose. Non, jusqu'en 1954, ce n'était pas encore développé dans l'intérieur. Mais c'est eux qui avaient la mainmise sur l'import-export à Saigon. C'est là où encore on va revenir à *L'Amant*. Alors là, je fais une parenthèse. La petite Marguerite Duras a eu le culot de raconter dans un roman autobiographique – récit très bref – qu'elle était très jolie et, qu'avec les années, elle a bu de l'alcool, elle s'est un peu abîmée. Elle le dit en toutes lettres ! [*JD imite* :] « J'étais jolie, oh ma chère, et l'alcool m'a abîmée ! », elle l'a dit, ha !

Alors quand elle avait 15 ans, elle était dans un collège huppé de Saigon et elle a rencontré un gros commerçant chinois bourré de fric et vicieux, qui a eu envie d'elle. Et elle, la petite idiote, est tombée dans ses bras. C'est *L'Amant*, c'est tout, c'est tout, point. Avec cela on fait un bouquin, un prix Goncourt et un film, hein ?

Par-dessus le marché elle ne sait même pas le vietnamien. Moi, le vietnamien, bon, je peux le déchiffrer, je peux exprimer quelques mots. Mais les langues de l'intérieur, je vous parle quatre dialectes couramment, couramment comme du français ! Et je continue à écrire. Des lettres privées avec des copains sré, jörai et autres. Ce sont des langues que je possède totalement.

AH – Revenons à Duras un moment ? Le roman qui m'a intéressé c'était *Le Barrage contre le Pacifique*.

JD – Non ! Il n'est pas bon. Il y a eu beaucoup mieux, surtout ses scénarios de films. Il y a *Hiroshima Mon Amour*, hein ? Excellent scénario. Resnais. Heureusement qu'elle a collaboré avec Resnais qui est un très grand bonhomme. Elle a du talent, il n'y a pas de doute.

AH – Elle a trop bu ? C'est l'alcool qui l'a ruinée ?

JD – Non elle n'a pas trop bu, elle ne sait pas boire. Moi je bois terriblement quand j'ai l'occasion. Je ne tremble même pas. Elle tremble. Complètement boursouflée. Comme Graham Greene. Je l'ai connu dans les années 1950. Il ne tremblait pas. Du gin, il en buvait tellement qu'il déconnait franchement. Une bouteille de gin pendant que je prends une seule limonade ! Complètement alcoolique. Pourtant j'aime beaucoup Graham Greene. J'aime beaucoup ce qu'il a fait. Je vais le mettre un peu à côté de Orwell. Pour moi, ce sont deux journalistes. Orwell a quand même fait des merveilles. Vous savez lequel je préfère d'Orwell ? *Animal Farm* ! C'est génial. Je l'ai traduit d'ailleurs. Qu'est-ce que je n'ai pas fait dans ma vie ! C'est très très fort, le cochon Napoléon, ha ! C'est terriblement anglais, c'est terriblement anarchiste, ça a tout pour me plaire.

[Pause]

AH – Comment le riz va des rizières jusqu'à Chợ Lớn ?

JD – Ça dépend des époques. Jusqu'en 1954, il y avait la consommation domestique et puis il y avait le ramasseur chinois qui prenait le surplus et qui allait le vendre sur le port de Saigon. Il habitait Chợ Lớn [et] il avait des petits Chinois qui travaillaient pour lui, qui allaient ramasser.

AH – Donc il avait tout un réseau en fait.

JD – C'était des réseaux tout ça, ce qu'on appelait les congrégations chinoises. C'est curieux, comme un nom religieux, il y avait quelque chose de secte ou de religieux aussi là-dedans. Ce qui est très marrant aussi, c'est que tous ces Chinois – qui n'étaient pas pour Tchang Kaï-chek, qui étaient encore moins pour Mao Tsé-toung – avaient dans leur maison le portrait de Sun Yat-sen. C'est ravissant, le père commun des deux branches.

Donc il y avait toujours des petits Chinois qui ramassaient le thé, le café, le riz, tout ce qu'il y avait à vendre sur Saigon. Ils apportent ça dans des gros entrepôts et puis les Chinois entreposaient. Quand il y avait un manque, ils bloquent l'entrepôt, les prix montaient, montaient… À ce moment-là ils débloquent et hop, ils les vendent !

J'ai vu un coup fumant avec des commerçants chinois dans le petit village de Choreo chez les Jörai. Ça c'est plus tard, 1955, 1956. À mon arrivée, il n'y avait que le village jörai, là, ma maison en bordure, la route et quelques commerçants vietnamiens. Des petites bricoles de rien du tout : des boîtes de conserves, de la Nestlé, des allumettes. Quelques Jörai ont essayé de faire un peu de commerce. Ça n'a pas marché du tout parce que les Jörai sont des philosophes, des artistes, des poètes, alors l'économie, elle a complètement bouché. Ils achetaient un truc à une piastre, ils voulaient le revendre à deux pour avoir immédiatement de l'argent. Évidemment, ça n'a pas marché du tout du tout. Alors les Vietnamiens se débrouillaient à peu près. [Mais] ils étaient insupportables avec moi. Ils me détestaient parce que je m'occupais des sauvages.

Arrivent quelques Chinois… Ils vendent à perte pendant un mois ou deux. Ce qui leur coûte deux piastres, ils revendaient une piastre. En deux mois ils ont coulé complètement les Vietnamiens. Ils sont les maîtres du marché. Ils font monter les prix comme ils veulent. Trois ans après, il y avait une école chinoise à Choreo devant le village pour tous ces *con* [= *enfants, JD parle vietnamien*] de Chinois qui étaient là ; ça grouillait, vous vous rendez compte ? C'est ça le Chinois : savoir vendre à perte pour couler l'autre. Ils ont réussi, ils ont coulé tout le monde, les Vietnamiens, les Jörai, ils ont tout coulé.

Comme ils ont leur congrégation à Saigon, il y a le capital derrière. Parce qu'admettons qu'une bouteille de Nestlé [s'achète pour] une piastre à Saigon. Plus le prix du transport, ça double à peu près : il y a deux jours de route. Ils le vendent 75 cents ! Moins cher qu'à Saigon. On se précipite ! En deux mois, ils ont complètement le monopole de toute la région. Après ça ils font les prix qu'ils veulent. Voilà le commerce local.

Local et international. C'est l'époque où il y avait encore les cargos, peut-être un par an, qui amenaient des produits en port de Saigon : français surtout, italiens, quelquefois anglais. Ça n'existe plus maintenant. Ils amenaient des caisses, des cargaisons et le Chinois il achetait la cargaison avant de savoir ce qu'il y avait dedans. Il achète tout le bateau. Les Français voulaient avoir ce qu'on appelle le connaissement –savoir ce qu'il y avait à bord – et puis acheter telle partie ou telle partie. Le Chinois se ramène là-dedans, le gros Chinois cossu, l'amant de Marguerite Duras, dit « moi, j'achète tout, tout ! ». Il savait très bien que c'était parfaitement vendable. Parce que les cargos de telle travée, ils vendaient pas de la cochonnerie : de la Nestlé, des bonnes conserves, un tas de choses, tabac, je ne sais pas quoi. Le Chinois achète tout le cargo. On débarque et ça va dans les entrepôts des Chinois à Chợ Lớn puis ils le gardent. Les demandes commencent à monter pour tel produit. Ils écoulent petit à petit. Quand ça devient la pénurie, alors hop ! Ils dégagent tout à des prix exorbitants. Ils ont fait des fortunes foireuses et ça, aucun Vietnamien n'a pu être de leur taille.

AH – Parce que les Vietnamiens avaient la même idée que les Jörai ?

JD – Oui, petit bénéfice immédiat. Parce que finalement le Vietnamien et le montagnard – je parle des paysans, des gens de l'intérieur, je ne parle pas des bourgeois, pas des citadins – ils sont tellement proches psychologiquement. Culturellement totalement différent, mais psychologiquement ils sont des petits exploitants de petits lopins de terre. Ils s'entraidaient bien sur place, pas de gros problèmes, pas d'animosité raciale, non non non. Les Vietnamiens bourgeois, citadins, communistes sont devenus racistes. Les racistes, ils traitent de « *mọi* » les sauvages des hauts plateaux, mes amis. Ce que les Grecs appelaient les *barbaroi*.

AH – Qu'est-ce qu'il y avait comme commerce entre villages ?

JD – Ça dépend. Entre Vietnamiens pas grand chose parce qu'ils ont les mêmes produits de leurs petites exploitations : quelques légumes, quelques maraîchers, des arbres fruitiers. À l'inverse, chez les montagnards, les moï, les Jörai, Sré et compagnie, c'est complètement spécialisé. Il y en a qui font des poteries, il y en a qui font des vanneries, il y en a qui font des tissages. Il y en a qui font de la forge, parce que le minerai de fer, ils forgent très très bien. Et on échange. Ça circule tout le temps, tout le temps là-dedans.

AH – Et c'est qui qui fait l'échange ?

JD – Les privés. Il n'y a pas de Chinois là-dedans. Ce sont des privés entre eux.

AH – Donc il n'y avait pas de métier de commerçant ?

JD – Du tout ! Du tout !

AH – Ils utilisaient une monnaie ?

JD – Non. Troc ! Ça n'existait pas la monnaie. Je parle des hauts plateaux, hein ?

AH – C'était sur une petite distance ?

JD – Oh… ça pouvait aller jusqu'à plus de 100 km ! Il y a des Jörai qui faisaient 200 km pour filer un buffle à des Lao, pour avoir une jarre ou un gong. 200 km !

AH – Parce qu'ils savent qu'il y a des jarres et des gongs là-bas ?

JD – Il n'y en a pas sur la partie Vietnam [de l'Indochine]. C'est de l'autre côté. Ils faisaient des grandes distances. Tous les montagnards des hauts plateaux qui allaient sur la côte – [à environ] 150 km [par] ce qu'on appelait les pistes du sel, toutes ces pistes qui allaient en direction à peu près ouest-est, des montagnes sur la côte – ils vendaient des cornes de rhinocéros, des cochons, des tissages, pour avoir du *nước mắm*, du sel, du poisson salé qu'ils ramenaient chez eux. Il y a des siècles que ça durait ce machin-là. C'est archi-connu, c'est raconté par beaucoup de littérateurs étrangers bien sûr. Ça circulait beaucoup et à l'amiable, gentiment, à qui volera le plus l'autre. Oui, évidemment, on est en Asie et on n'a pas de carnet des comptes, de chèques. On se roule, on se roule. Alors ça marchait très bien. Parce que sur la côte, il y avait de quoi vendre aux Chinois ou ailleurs – je parle des Vietnamiens de la côte – et puis à l'intérieur, il y avait du sel, du poisson, du *nước mắm* et cetera.

AH – Ils se déplaçaient comment ?

JD – À pied, mais à pied ! Si on traîne des cochons derrière soi, il ne faut pas une semaine pour aller des hauts plateaux sur la côte. Si on va en marche forcée, on peut le faire en trois jours. 150 km ce n'est pas terrible, mais hop-hop hop-hop. Je l'ai fait à pied.

AH – Qu'est-ce qu'ils ont comme chaussures ?

JD – Ils [n'en] n'ont pas. Les Vietnamiens non plus, je parle de ceux de la campagne. Tout le monde est pieds nus. On suit des pistes. Quand on sort des pistes alors à ce moment-là on met des espèces de petites sandales avec des pneus et des trucs comme ça, à cause du rotin. Le rotin est une liane, plus grosse que le pouce, avec des épines horribles tous les 10 cm et ça court sur le sol. Alors si on marche sur des épines de rotin, aargh ! Sur les pistes on va pieds nus. Elles ont été foulées par tellement de gens. Tout le monde est pieds nus, moi je suis encore pieds nus ! Je me demande comment on peut se fourrer les pieds dans des chaussures qui font tellement mal. Le pied est comme la main, ça commence mince et ça se termine large. Et des chaussures, c'est juste l'inverse, ça commence large et ça termine mince. Alors votre pied dans une chaussure, c'est une absurdité totale !

AH – Il y avait des dangers de voleurs ?

JD – Oui. Les Jörai en particulier étaient réputés pour [être] des voleurs merveilleux. Ils volent des chevaux. Jamais de riz, oh la la ! C'est sacré, on n'a pas le droit d'y toucher. Les greniers à riz sont à l'extérieur du village, personne n'y touche jamais. Si jamais il y avait eu un vol de riz, ce serait un tollé, ce serait la mise à mort, c'est effroyable. Je n'en connais pas de cas de vol de riz. En dehors de ça, ça volait, ça volait, oui, copieusement. Mais alors, il se trouve que moi j'avais une case qui n'avait pas de porte. Il m'arrivait de partir trois ou quatre jours en tournée. Ça restait grand ouvert, on ne m'a jamais rien volé. J'ai fait exprès même une ou deux fois de laisser quelques piastres vietnamiennes en vue, comme ça sur mon bureau, qui était par terre. Je rentre au bout de quatre-cinq jours, rien touché. On était rentré seulement pour faire la poussière, des amis qui venaient nettoyer, oui ! Ils ont vu, ils ont laissé.

AH – [Et] sur les pistes ?

JD – Oh, on n'est pas en Chine. Il n'y a pas de bandits, il n'y a pas de pirates, il n'y a pas de brigands, rien sur les pistes. Il peut y avoir le tigre, au plus. Enfin le tigre est tellement froussard, quand il sent l'homme, il fout le camp. Il faut vraiment qu'il soit affamé pour attaquer. C'est le plus grand froussard du monde le tigre. La panthère est plus agressive parce qu'elle peut aller sur les arbres et puis tuk ! elle vous tombe dessus. En gros il n'y avait aucun danger, jamais d'attaque. C'est le pays le plus calme du monde.

AH – [Les montagnards] participent à l'économie des Viet ?

JD – Oh très localement, sur des petits marchés. Ils amènent une hotte d'oranges pour avoir en échange un petit corsage, des trucs comme ça. Évidemment au sens large du terme, ça rentre dans l'économie, mais c'est tellement insignifiant dans le commerce vietnamien. Autrefois, c'était plus important, quand il n'y avait pas d'Européens, pas de commerce extérieur à la péninsule indochinoise. Alors là, les Vietnamiens, qui n'étaient encore que sur la côte, avaient beaucoup d'échanges avec les populations de l'intérieur qui descendaient avec des cochons, avec des défenses d'éléphant, avec des cornes de rhinocéros, avec du bois de cannelle pour avoir du poisson, du *nước mắm*, des trucs comme ça… Ça fonctionnait beaucoup beaucoup.

Un peu plus tard, il y a eu quelques colporteurs annamites – c'est comme ça qu'on les appelait à l'époque – qui montaient sur les plateaux pour vendre des bricoles dans les villages ; j'en ai vu encore. [À] un moment, tout à fait de mèche avec les Viet Minh, les colporteurs qui passaient partout vendaient des bonbons empoisonnés, de l'alcool empoisonné. Il y a eu des centaines de morts chez les Jörai. Pour les liquider ! Parce que tous les Vietnamiens de tous bords, de Saigon, de Hanoi, du maquis ou du gouvernement n'avaient qu'une idée : se débarrasser des montagnards. Ça, ça a duré assez longtemps.

AH – C'était quand ?

JD – Dans les années 1968, par là. J'ai quitté en 1970.

Bon, je vois que le soir tombe, je vais faire la bouffe pour les chiens…

[Pause]

JD – J'aimerai savoir où vous en êtes.

AH – J'avais deux idées en tête. L'une c'était de faire les structures de l'économie et l'autre c'est de mettre en relation ces structures avec un certain nombre de conjonctures dans le temps. Les conjonctures étant la crise économique, la reprise après la crise, la deuxième guerre mondiale, la guerre française, en commençant en 1930, en terminant en 1954. On commence avec le Vietnam en pleine prospérité des années 1920 et puis on finit avec la fin de la guerre, les Français qui se retirent et la division du Vietnam.

JD – À mon avis il serait bon d'étudier l'économie vietnamienne, culturellement vietnamienne en tant que telle, avant toute intrusion des étrangers. Alors là, ce n'est pas de la tarte. Quelle était l'économie vietnamienne avant 1859 ? Dans les grandes lignes, il y avait la commune, les mandarins et l'empereur, un système confucéen. Il faut bien connaître l'aspect économique du Confucianisme. Ce n'est pas si évident que ça [mais] sans ça on ne peut rien savoir de l'économie vietnamienne avant l'intrusion des étrangers. Et encore, parce que si la prise de Saigon [est] en

1859, il y a eu sous Louis XIV des Français qui se sont introduits et avant il y avait des Portugais. Alors les Français étaient nuls pour le commerce et juste bons à faire des forts à la Vauban [mais] les Portugais s'entendaient davantage sur le commerce. Ils ont du donc profondément – les Portugais surtout – modifier l'économie vietnamienne, ouverture de ports et cetera.

Il faut remonter plus loin encore, au XIIe siècle à peu près, [avec] l'arrivée des Arabes. Une bonne partie du Champa est devenue musulmane ; la côte était commercialement colonisée par les Arabes. Ça remonte très loin cette histoire-là. Donc, l'économie vietnamienne – si jamais il y en a eu une originale, parce qu'avant elle était chinoise – a été modifiée par tous ces apports étrangers. À se débrouiller là-dedans, il faut être vraiment économiste, historien...

Je ne peux rien vous dire de plus, je vous ai dit tout ce que je savais, c'est-à-dire rien ! Ce n'est pas mon problème, je n'ai jamais travaillé là-dessus.

AH – La seule économie vietnamienne, c'est l'économie villageoise ?

JD – On peut l'étudier à ce niveau. Parce que, pas plus les Chinois que les Arabes et par la suite les Portugais et par la suite les Français, ils n'ont pas pénétré les villages. [Ils ont] contacté les mandarins, les empereurs, les grands chefs, rien au niveau du village. S'il est vrai que le Vietnam soit un pays de villages, l'économie du village est peut-être une clé pour comprendre la victoire de 1975.

AH – Les Américains, il fallait détruire chaque village, parce qu'à détruire la moitié des villages du delta...

JD – Ça ne sert à rien.

AH – ...il y a toujours l'autre moitié qui fonctionne. Et vous pouvez détruire autant que vous voulez...

JD – ...il y en a un autre juste à côté. C'est comme dans les mythes. Vous coupez la tête du serpent et il en pousse sept nouvelles. C'est une des forces du Vietnam parce que malgré toutes les apparences, mandarinales, impériales, confucianistes..., c'est relativement anarchique : il n'y a pas de pouvoir supérieur, chacun se débrouille dans son coin. Pour une rébellion le Viet Minh, c'était la perle, la trouvaille. Ils ont joué là-dessus et c'est ça qui a fait gagner. Parce qu'il n'y a pas de pouvoir. Parce que la petite économie villageoise, petite communauté [est] très limitée, très fermée. On ne connaissait même pas le mandarin : on ne parlait pas de l'empereur, mais même pas du mandarin qui est au-dessus. Quand un système comme le Stalinisme nationaliste hanoïen peut s'infiltrer là-dedans, il y a des points partout sur la carte du ravitaillement des troupes. [Il n'y a] personne qui va le contrecarrer par pouvoir. Le petit village jouait sur l'anarchie.

Il fallait un Vietnamien comme Ho Chi Minh pour le sentir. C'est vraiment génial et ça a fonctionné. On doit aussi les mettre en relation avec d'autres phénomènes d'impérialisme stalinisant, comme en Russie d'ailleurs. Chacun se débrouillait dans son petit coin, il n'y a pas de pouvoir central. Des petits sous-fifres secondaires cherchent des impôts qui restent dans la poche des sous-fifres. Mais le Tsar n'est au courant de rien, comme l'empereur au Vietnam n'est au courant de rien. Le mandarin au Vietnam, à l'époque, il n'était au courant de rien, il s'en moquait.

Mais ce qui me met peu à l'aise, c'est que non seulement je ne suis pas économiste – je ne connais rien à l'économie – mais ça ne m'intéresse absolument pas. Ce qui m'intéresse, c'est la culture, les techniques, la littérature orale, les mythes et les gens, les épopées, tout ce que ces gens racontent et ce qu'ils peuvent penser. Alors l'économie, pfzz ! Ils ont eu évidemment une économie, économie d'échange, de troc, une économie socialement. C'est un tout autre monde.

Puis par-dessus le marché, les Vietnamiens je n'y connais rien. J'ai vécu dedans comme une coquille St-Jacques, on se fout du milieu. J'étais dans ma coquille : les Vietnamiens, pfzz ! La guerre, je m'en foutais. Que les Viets, les Français, les Américains, les Chinois, les n'importe quoi se battent entre eux, pfzz ! J'étais absolument le type des minorités. J'étais complètement en dehors de ça.

Ah oui, les Vietnamiens, pfzz ! Je n'y connais rien. L'économie, ce n'est pas mon secteur. Mon intérêt principal, c'était la culture. Je parle de valeurs intellectuelles, religieuses, mystiques, poétiques, qu'on trouve dans la littérature orale, les mythes, les légendes, des poèmes. C'est là-dessus que je veux surtout travailler. Le reste je m'en fous. L'économie je m'en fous ; ça, c'est mon économie. Tout ce que j'ai écrit sur les populations parmi lesquelles j'ai vécu et sur lesquelles j'ai travaillé va dans le sens que je viens de vous dire : des valeurs culturelles de qualité universelle.

AH – Mais les valeurs des gens ont quand même un regard sur l'économique. Quand on parle des valeurs de la réflexion, ils réfléchissent à gagner leur pain.

JD – Dans le secteur que je connais, la littérature, il n'y a pas cette réflexion. On ne peut rien en tirer, à moins de faire dire aux textes ce qu'ils ne disent pas. Non, rien. C'est torpeureux, c'est poétique, c'est du rêve, c'est de l'ailleurs, c'est de la grande poésie ! C'est comme si vous me demandiez s'il y a une dimension économique à la chanson de Roland. Ou encore pire dans le roman du Graale : l'économie moderne dans le roman du Graale. C'est à se taper le derrière par terre ! On est complètement au-delà dans le Graale.

AH – On ne se préoccupe pas du quotidien, en fait.

JD – Non seulement ça, on fait exprès d'aller ailleurs.

AH – Pour échapper…

JD – Ce n'est pas pour échapper. Pour rigoler. Une échappatoire, ça voudrait dire qu'on voudrait fuir quelque chose. On n'a rien à fuir. Le quotidien, on le vit – entre rêves – mais ce n'est pas une valeur. Le riz, ce n'est pas une valeur. Et cuir du riz, ce n'est pas une valeur. C'est une nécessité, comme on va faire caca, hein ? Tous les jours je bouffe mon riz, tous les jours je fais caca, tous les jours je bouffe mon piment, c'est des trucs mécaniques, biologiques, on s'en fout. C'est naturel, c'est simple, on n'en parle pas, ça n'a aucun intérêt.

Quand on est libre le soir, la nuit, ou quand il pleut trop, on ne peut pas aller se balader dehors, on boit ! On invente un tas de belles choses, le Graale, chanson de Roland, Tristan et Iseult. Les côtés de l'économique là-dedans, c'est de l'anti-économique justement. C'est du gratuit. C'est la création pure et la création est gratuite par définition.

Vous enregistrez ?

AH – Oui.

JD – Ça vous pourrez le garder parce que c'est un sacré morceau que je vous ai donné là. Je le crois très fort. C'est ça qui m'intéresse, le gratuit.

Alors les économistes, quand je vois *Le Monde* par exemple, je lis la première page, quelquefois la seconde, rarement la dernière. Mais quand je vois trois-quatre pages à l'intérieur, « Économie », ça va immédiatement dans le poêle pour allumer mon feu. Je suis complètement allergique à l'économie. Parce que c'est exactement l'inverse de la gratuité et la création littéraire c'est exactement la gratuité. Ça ne sert à rien, ça ne rapporte pas un sou à tous ces gens-là d'avoir inventé des mythes extraordinaires. Au Moyen Âge, il n'y avait pas de droits d'auteur, hein ? Les auteurs de Tristan et Iseult, de la quête du Graale, du roi Arthur et cetera, n'ont jamais touché un sou là-dessus.

Quand je traduis leurs mythes et que je peux les publier, je leur envoie du fric. Mais ils n'y pensaient même pas. Ils ne comprennent même pas que d'avoir conté un truc merveilleux, ça peut rapporter du fric. Moi c'est pour les remercier, parce que je n'ai jamais payé un informateur. Je n'avais pas d'informateurs, j'avais des amis. Je n'ai jamais donné un sou à qui que ce soit. D'ailleurs là-bas je n'avais pas un rond, maintenant ça recommence, je n'ai pas un rond. Quand j'étais au CNRS, je pouvais un peu me débrouiller, j'ai publié. Alors de temps en temps, j'essayais de dédommager, d'envoyer. Ils ne comprennent pas ! C'est gratuit, on ne paie pas quelque chose qui est gratuit ! C'est une injure presque : je vous fais un cadeau et vous me donnez de l'argent en échange de mon cadeau. Un conteur qui me raconte une épopée magnifique qui dure quatre-cinq heures, ce serait une injure que de lui donner quoique ce soit. C'est la giclée de la gratuité.

Donc je suis anti-économique comme je suis anarchiste, caque ! Oh il est méchant le monsieur, hein ? Oh la la la, ses chiens sont plus gentils, hein ? Ha ha ! Non mais je suis comédien, vous savez. Je sais très bien que j'ai joué la comédie. Je fais exprès, je sais ce que je fais, ça m'amuse et en même temps il y a quelque chose à en tirer.

[Pause]

J'ai fait pas mal de grec. Je me défends davantage en latin, un petit peu en hébreu, mais en grec, quand même ! Je préfère le Grec au Romain, tout simplement parce que je préfère un artiste à un épicier. Je préfère un conférencier éloquent à un avocat de bas étage. Je préfère les temples grecs de Delphes ou d'Athènes, le Parthénon, d'autres, au Colisée, qui est chiant, qu'on revoit à Nîmes ou qu'on revoit ailleurs, pour des courses de taureaux, pour que les gens se tuent les uns les autres. C'est plein de sang les colisées. C'est des brutes les Romains, des brutes !

AH – Ils ont eu leur Muraille de Chine aussi, les Romains, pour les barbares.

JD – Non ils faisaient mieux, ils faisaient mieux. Ils ne faisaient pas de murailles, ils faisaient des routes. Oh il n'y a pas de murailles, ils faisaient des routes avec des pierres grandes comme ça. Il y en a encore des traces un peu partout en Europe, jusqu'en Angleterre.

AH – Et la muraille, c'est en Angleterre.

JD – Oui, les Anglais, ils ont toujours inventé ces trucs-là, ha ha !

Voyez justement, c'est marrant, mais il y a quand même un entrecoupement de choses. Vous opposez les Athéniens avec les Romains et puis les économistes et les artistes. Les Romains sont des économistes et les Grecs sont des artistes. Et moi, je me mets du côté des artistes. Bon, j'ai le droit, hein ? Les économistes, je n'aime même pas les voir en peinture, pas plus que les sociologues, pas plus que les ethnologues, parce que trop souvent ils parlent de ce qu'ils ne savent pas. C'est tellement facile ! Qui va leur donner tort, hein ? Puis l'économie pour moi c'est les sous, c'est la banque, c'est les actions... ça me donne une éruption. Je ne peux pas supporter que ça rapporte de l'argent, qu'on joue, les jeux d'argent, tout ça, c'est horrible. Quand je pense que ça m'arrive entre deux émissions à la radio de tomber sur une cochonnerie de jeu télévisé, *Roue de la Fortune* ou une cochonnerie de ce genre-là. Alors là, l'économie et l'argent, il ne faut pas m'en parler. Mais non, c'est monstrueux, monstrueux.

Je suis de l'autre côté, carrément de l'autre côté et ce n'est pas des racines culturelles de chez moi. Parce que je suis fils de haut bourgeois, j'avais beaucoup d'argent. C'est venu au contact des sauvages. C'est eux qui m'ont cultivé. Oui ! Ils m'ont appris des valeurs que j'ignorais. On peut être dans la boue de la rizière, on peut faire des travaux idiots qu'on n'aime pas, il faut bien bouffer. Et il y a un moment où ça sort et on libre, on est soi et puis on invente, on crée, on fait des poèmes. Ils m'ont révélé ça, qu'on pouvait créer en sortant de sa merde, tout en y étant toujours. Et ça c'est fort. Pour moi, ces populations ont plus d'attrait. On les tue bien sûr, c'est très gênant. On fait tout pour les tuer. On a tellement peur de la création, parce que la création est anarchique par définition. On crée, donc on sort des normes, donc c'est anarchique, alors ils suppriment. Et le Vietnam le fait avec ses minorités, et la Russie l'a fait avec des milliers de peuples jusqu'au fin fond de la Sibérie, les liquider et les remplacer par les Slaves. On parle des Amazoniens : le cher Christophe Colombe, il n'était pas responsable. Il était... comme Boudarel, ha ha ! Du même ordre : il part sur un faux idéal :

> « De Palos de Moguer,
> routiers et capitaines
> partaient ivres
> d'un rêve héroïque et brutal ».[1]

Ils ne sont pas comme les autres, ils inventent, ils sont artistes. En supprimant, on supprime tous ceux qui ont le culot, le toupet, l'audace de vouloir créer, sortir – pas s'évader – sortir, monter, aller voir autre chose.

Vous voyez, dans un village jörai, une quinzaine de personnes dans la case, c'est spontané, un conteur se met à commencer une épopée. Il exprime un « non-encore pensé » qui était un peu chez tout le monde et qu'il fait surgir comme ça, par son organe : la voix ! C'est un comédien, un conteur. Et l'organe, il faut l'entendre. J'ai des enregistrements d'une beauté, par la langue, par son organe, qui charme. Et il dit ce qu'il y a en-dessous, ce qu'il y a dedans, ce qu'il y a dans tous les cœurs qui sont là, les gosses comme les vieux. Au bout d'une heure de conte, les gosses s'endorment parce qu'il n'y a pas de conte pour enfants, il n'y a pas de conte pour vieillards. Tout le monde est là, tout le monde prend ce qu'il peut. Les gosses sont endormis, les vieux un peu plus tard, les femmes les

---

1. Dournes cite José Maria de Heredia, « Les conquérants », dans Les Trophées (1893) : « Comme un vol de gerfauts hors du charnier natal, Fatigués de porter leurs misères hautaines, De Palos de Moguer, routiers et capitaines Partaient, ivres d'un rêve héroïque et brutal. »

dernières : elles sont coriaces, elles ne dorment pas beaucoup. Il y a des conteuses aussi. Ça, c'est extraordinaire.

C'est ce que j'appelle l'économie de ces populations-là. Ha ha ! Je renverse complètement le problème, exprès ! C'est leur économie. Ça marche encore. Il y a 22 ans que je les ai quittés, ils m'écrivent encore. Dans la dernière lettre, ils disaient « vous vous intéressiez vachement à nos contes – nous aussi on s'est mis à s'y intéresser – si vous en voulez on va vous envoyer encore des textes ». Ce n'est pas génial, ça ?

Bah ! C'est leur économie. Je renverse complètement les données. L'économie ce n'est pas les sous, ce n'est pas le grain de riz, ce n'est pas l'huile d'arachide. L'économie, *oikosnomia*. « *Oikos* » c'est la maison, « *nomia* » c'est la règle. C'est du grec, la « règle de la maison ». Chacun a ses règles. Les Romains, c'est des épiciers. Les Grecs étaient des tragédiens. Les Jörai et d'autres sont des conteurs de légendes, artistes et musiciens. C'est leur économie – *oikosnomia* – la règle de la maison. C'est comme ça que ça se règle les affaires.

Là, justement, on règle les différends de justice et tout ça, c'est génial chez eux. On chante, on récite en chantant des versets qu'ils ont telle affaire : « s'il y a ceci, il y a cela – s'il y a cela, il y a ceci, et cetera, et cetera ». Ça dure des heures, c'est tellement beau qu'à la fin tout le monde dit d'accord et le différend, il est réglé. C'est fini, on n'en parle plus, pas de prison, pas de juge, pas d'amande, pas de dette, rien. On boit un bon coup et puis c'est fini. Parce qu'on a fait ça avec leur oikosnomia, le règlement de la maison, par la voix, par la parole, par invention, en raboutant des textes, à qui parlera le mieux. Voilà mon économie.

Alors là je quitte la voix du comédien pour prendre la voix du vieux frère, pour vous donner un conseil : ne limitez pas votre économie à des sous, hmm ? Ça va loin ce que je dis. Essayez de vous pencher un peu sur l'économie des gens qui n'ont pas d'économie au sens moderne occidental du mot.

Mais il y a un bouquin à faire là-dessus : une autre économie, hein ? Économie de mots aussi. On va jouer sur les mots, en comédien. Avec trois mots on vous exprime une foule de choses, parce qu'il n'y a rien de plus condensé que la littérature orale. Il ne faut pas croire que ce sont des trucs qui se répètent, qui se répètent, qui se rallongent, qui se raboutent. En trois mots on vous dit plein de choses. Un exemple, une devinette en quatre mots, quatre monosyllabes : « *Âko' hơoñ tung čum* ». *Âko'*, la tête – *hơoñ*, caresse – *tung*, le cul – *čum*, baiser. C'est splendide ! C'est la pipe. Le dernier gosse jörai sait ça. Comme économie de moyens, hein ? Économie de paroles, économie de mots. Vous n'avez pas pensé à cette dimension de l'économie, ce n'est pas génial ?

J'ai tout appris là-bas, qu'est-ce que vous voulez ! J'avais de bons profs quand j'étais au lycée mais enfin jamais à ce degré-là. Ça fait revoir toutes les notions qu'on avait avant. Avec quatre monosyllabes qui jouent sur les mots bien sûr, parce qu'on veut que ce soit choquant. Caresser, baiser, hein ? Ils sont très sensuels par-dessus le marché. Quel humour, quelle économie, quatre monosyllabes ! Il y a toute une philosophie là-dedans. Ça veut dire « baiser, caresser, culotter, c'est la rigolade, une bonne bouffée, ça vaut mieux ». Il y a ça aussi dedans. Non, je n'avais jamais appris de trucs pareils.

Je travaille sur l'architecture… Regardez encore la construction, comme économie de moyens, ce n'est pas cochon. Quelques bouts de bambou, quelques bouts de bois et on fait une maison qui résiste à toutes les tempêtes. Et ça je l'ai vu dans les villages. Les maisons sur pilotis. À côté de ça, les Vietnamiens qui avaient des cases en pisé, au ras du sol. Un typhon : les Vietnamiens… plus rien ! Les cases jörai faisaient ça [JD mime] – j'étais dedans – elles faisaient ça, typhon passé, claque, bouge plus et ça ne coûte rien.

AH – Et c'est ça l'économie aussi, la forêt ?

JD – Bon, là encore, j'aurai long à dire. Très long à dire, parce que je me suis battu avec des botanistes, pédologues, géologues, tous les -logues que vous voulez, -logue machin-chose, -logue machin-chouette… Bref. On a dit que ces populations détruisaient la forêt. Ça marche toujours ?

AH – Oui.

JD – Elle est interminable, votre bande. J'avais bien fait de vous dire d'apporter un truc, hein ? Parce que je ne peux pas le répéter, j'invente au fur et à mesure. Oui ! Parce qu'il y a deux sortes de comédien. Il y a ceux qui ont un texte qu'ils ont appris et puis ceux qui créent complètement leur texte. Je suis de ceux-là.

AH – Et qui l'oublient…

JD – …immédiatement après. Non, je ne peux pas l'oublier parce que je l'avais en tête avant. Il n'était pas prononcé, je l'avais en tête. Je le sors. Il revient en tête et je pourrais le ressortir autrement, d'une autre façon, dans d'autres circonstances.

J'en reviens à l'économie de la forêt. La technique de l'essartage, ça suppose une faible densité de population au kilomètre carré. Donc c'est un grand luxe qu'on peut se permettre dans des régions où il n'y a personne. En quoi ça consiste ? À délimiter un périmètre de forêt. Abattre d'abord la broussaille ensuite abattre les gros arbres, qui en tombant écrasent tout ce qu'on avait à moitié abattu avant ; bien nettoyer. On y met le feu. Avec des pare-feux tout autour, j'ai assisté, j'ai participé, hein ! Le feu ne passe pas à un mètre des pare-feux. Des pare-feux parfaits. On met le feu là-dedans. C'est au mois d'avril, à la fin de la saison sèche. Parce qu'en mai il commence à pleuvoir un petit peu. Sur les cendres, avec le bâton à fouir – fouir c'est faire un trou – on met des grains. Du riz, du maïs, des courges, tout mélangé. Là-dessus, fin mai, juin, juillet, août, septembre même, ça pleut. Il faut juste désherber un petit peu. Octobre, c'est à peu près la fin des pluies. Novembre, on récolte, on récolte, on récolte, de quoi bouffer pendant presque une année. Puis du vachement bon riz, pas la cochonnerie que vous avez bouffée à Hanoi. C'est le meilleur possible, le riz d'essart. Vous savez que le riz c'est une plante normalement aquatique mais il était depuis je ne sais pas combien de siècles, sinon des millénaires, acclimaté à des terrains secs, qui reçoivent beaucoup de pluie. Cet essart on le cultive pendant deux ans, trois ans maximum, parce qu'après la terre va s'épuiser. On ne met pas d'engrais, c'est dans les cendres. Bon ça épuise. Qu'est-ce qu'on fait ? On en prend un autre à côté.

Je vous donne un exemple. Dans le village de Choreo, en pays de Jörai, où j'étais et où j'ai construit ma cagna ('cagna', c'est un mot Vietnamien, *cái nhà*, ça veut dire la maison, ce n'est pas du tout péjoratif). J'ai construit ma cagna sur un ancien essart, abandonné depuis dix ans. Il y avait des arbres de 20 centimètres de diamètre. Il ne faut pas dire que la pratique du brûlis détruit la forêt, ça pousse comme du chiendent. Bon, j'ai abattu un certain nombre de ces arbres pour faire ma maison, et pour les remplacer par des arbres fruitiers. J'ai enlevé des espèces qui n'étaient pas utiles et j'ai mis des arbres fruitiers à la place, des mangues et des trucs comme ça. Le brûlis ne détruit pas du tout, bah !

Donc voilà l'économie de forêt de ces populations. On coupe rigoureusement ce qu'il faut. C'est la même chose pour couper un arbre pour en faire une maison. On ne va pas en couper dix si on en a besoin d'un. On coupe un. Quand on va à la chasse, on ne va pas tuer dix cerfs comme font les Français. Ils ne peuvent même pas les bouffer, ça pourrit. On en tue un à la rigueur, pour nourrir tout un village pendant un mois. C'est économique et au sens ancien du mot. L'économie, c'est tout, parce qu'on n'a rien, on est pauvre. Les grands économes sont des pauvres. Des vrais pauvres, pas les pauvres qui vont au supermarché et qui achètent à crédit, même les bagnoles. Même les gosses ont chacun leur bagnole, trois-quatre bagnoles par maison. Ce sont des faux pauvres.

Alors à côté de ça, l'économie américaine au Vietnam. Pour eux la forêt c'est là que sont tous les Viet Minh. Alors justement, je l'ai vu, hein ! D'abord du défoliant, très dangereux pour les hommes. J'ai eu un copain missionnaire qui a été grièvement brûlé, immobilisé pour la vie, simplement parce qu'il a reçu une giclée de 20 km de là. C'était un avion à haute altitude. J'ai eu dans mon jardin, à plus de 20 km du passage de l'avion, du maïs qui était crochu comme ça. À 20 km. Voilà l'économie américaine : défoliant ! Un bon passage de défoliant puis il ne sortira plus rien. Là-dessus, napalm. Je l'ai vu, j'ai des témoignages, j'ai même des rapports officiels de l'ONU. Il faudra plusieurs siècles avant que la forêt indochinoise puisse repartir, si elle repart jamais.

Les Américains commençaient à désertifier le Vietnam et les Vietnamiens continuent ! Sur ce qu'il reste de cette forêt, ils passent au bulldozer. Mais je l'ai vu ça aussi. Des jardins – des moï, pas des Vietnamiens – au bulldozer, vrooom, on arrache tout. Par-dessus le marché quand ces braves montagnards faisaient des essarts ou des jardins, ils laissaient toujours par-ci par-là un arbre [contre] l'érosion, pour retenir le sol. Dans ces zones tropicales il y a peut-être 20 cm de terre cultivable. En dessous c'est mauvais. Bon alors, bulldozer : les Vietnamiens continuent l'œuvre américaine, mais copieusement. Les bulldozers, comme les avions, c'est piqué aux Américains qui ont foutu le camp à une vitesse. Ils ont tout laissé, les Américains, tout ! Ils sont partis comme des lapins. Les Vietnamiens ramassaient tout ça, ils ont continué. On démolit tout, la forêt, tchouk ! Dans dix ans, le Vietnam sera Sahara et voilà ! Les montagnards, ils n'ont plus qu'à crever, parce qu'eux, c'était économique.

AH – Qu'est-ce qu'ils font les montagnards ?

JD – Ah ils se plaignent, ils ne peuvent rien faire, ils sont reconnus par personne.

AH – Je veux dire, économiquement, pour manger.

JD – Ils font des petits jardins.

AH – Ils ne peuvent plus faire des essarts ?

JD – Il n'y a plus rien à brûler, ce qui n'a pas brûlé était rasé au bulldozer. Parce que pour le Vietnamien, l'économie c'est… comme les Russes, ils ont piqué ça aux Russes : le rendement immédiat. Et c'est comme ça qu'on a tué la mer d'Aral.

J'ai vu le même coup au Vietnam, à 20 km en aval du village où j'étais, sur le grand fleuve Apa. Il y avait des géologues, des Hollandais, un tas de gens – c'était entre 1954 et 1975, vous voyez – qui sont venus pour étudier des problèmes, pour faire des champs de coton. Ils ont repéré un coin au bord du fleuve pour faire le coton. Chose curieuse, il n'y avait aucun établissement de Jörai là-dessus. Les spécialistes, les techniciens, les experts et tout ça, ils étaient obligés de passer par chez moi…

[Pause]

Contre tous mes avis, contre l'avis des experts amis jörai, le gouvernement réuni décide de faire un immense champ de coton. On installe des Vietnamiens, on installe plein de maisons, des champs. Quelques mois après, crue du fleuve ! Les Jörai ils le savaient, c'est pour ça ils n'ont jamais même fait un jardin là-dessus. Le coton, les maisons, les

Vietnamiens, tout est parti vers la mer. Et voilà, on n'en parlait plus, liquidé. Ça c'est un procédé russe, c'est un procédé vietnamien, c'est un procédé mondial. C'est ce qu'on appelle l'économie ! Alors que moi, j'ai le culot de soutenir l'économie des sauvages qui protègent la nature. Ils ne détruisent pas pour détruire, juste pour vivre. Exactement comme un tigre : s'il a besoin d'une proie, il en bouffe une, pas dix. Pas plus malin que le tigre, il va détruire juste ce qu'il faut, pas plus. Et par-dessus le marché alors – ça c'est le comble du comble – quand un Jörai abat un arbre, il lui demande pardon avant ! Voilà, j'en suis là. On taille un rosier, on demande pardon au rosier de couper une branche. J'ai peur de faire mal. Ça, c'est sauvage. Ça, c'est économique.

AH – Reste-t-il des montagnards, des peuples au Laos, en Chine, en Birmanie qui pratiquent toujours l'essart ?

JD – Ça va être difficile de répondre. Depuis trop d'années je suis coupé de tout renseignement.

[Le] Laos c'est maintenant devenu une colonie vietnamienne, comme les Vietnamiens voulaient faire au Cambodge. Parce que les Vietnamiens s'estiment les héritiers de l'Indochine française. J'ai vu dans les années 1960 des cahiers d'écolier des écoles vietnamiennes dans la région gouvernée par Saigon, pas par Hanoi. Vous savez que dans les cahiers d'écolier, il y a une carte du Vietnam : Vietnam, Laos, Cambodge, de la même couleur ! Et voilà !

Quand les Français sont allés s'installer au Laos et au Cambodge, ils ont pris des Vietnamiens avec eux. Ce sont les Français qui ont introduit les premiers Vietnamiens au Laos, les premiers Vietnamiens sur les hauts plateaux. Parce qu'il était impensable pour un Français d'avoir comme chauffeur de son automobile ou comme cuisinier un sauvage aux pieds nus. Il lui fallait un Vietnamien bien civilisé, bien policé.

[Maintenant les Vietnamiens] ont déjà bouffé le Laos, complètement. Ils étaient sur le point de bouffer le Cambodge [quand] il y a eu l'affaire Pol Pot, conquête militaire par le Vietnam, régime de collaboration de Heng Samrin. Maintenant il y a Norodom Sihanouk, le grand comédien, qui essaie de revenir sur la scène. Je ne peux pas vous dire ce qui se passe au

Laos ou au Vietnam. Sinon que bon, l'essartage est interdit et le bulldozer est toléré. Voilà l'économie !

Alors les populations véritablement économes, les autochtones… Là encore il y a un truc : « autochtone » ça veut dire les gens qui sont de la terre. La terre c'est la leur, ils la respectent. Il n'y a pas de document écrit disant que c'est à eux mais depuis des millénaires c'est à eux. Ils le savent et ils lui rendent grâce, à la terre. Elle les nourrit, ils la respectent. L'économie. Voilà la politique des uns, respecter leur terre. La politique des autres, les économistes mondiaux, c'est de la leur arracher. Il n'y a pas d'écrits, pas de textes : cette terre est à personne. Et donc au gouvernement, au pouvoir en place, de s'occuper de ces terres. En particulier les Vietnamiens qui arrivent sur les hauts plateaux : ce n'est pas leur terre, ils s'en foutent, ils détruisent tout, ils cassent tout, ce n'est pas à eux. Le rendement immédiat : ils ont obtenu, ils ont tout coupé, tout bousillé, pendant un an ou deux, pour faire des légumes, des choux, des trucs comme ça, puis abandonner après quelques années. C'est authentique, je l'ai vu aussi. Ce n'est pas leur terre, ils s'en foutent ! Voilà, ce n'est pas leur terre, ils ne sont pas chez eux, on détruit à ce moment-là.

À la différence des Français. C'est vraiment l'opposé. Pour eux c'était leur terre, le Vietnam, l'Indochine. C'était à eux, par droit de conquête, tout ce qu'on veut, c'était à eux. Ils la respectaient, la terre. Ils ne détruisaient rien. Opposition complète des Français et des Américains. Le Français en fait sa terre : beaucoup de colons et des planteurs étaient des paysans ! Ils savent ce que c'est que la terre, on la respecte la terre, on ne détruit pas. Les Américains, il n'y a pas de terre, il n'y a pas de peuple, il n'y a rien. Il fallait faire table rase, pour faire un *nomansland* entre les Philippines et la Chine, pour qu'ils aient des points d'appui solides en Sud-est asiatique. Pour le Français c'était sacré. J'en ai rencontré beaucoup de ces colons. J'en avais croisé des impossibles, des petits colons. Comme ils abusaient des montagnards, coolies et tout ! Mais c'était leur terre…

AH – Ils s'y étaient investis.

JD – Enracinés ! Enracinés ! Un fonctionnaire restait deux ans, trois ans maximum. Le colon restait toute sa vie, tous les dix ans un retour en France à tout casser. Ça montre le respect de la terre.

L'autochtone, les indigènes, aborigènes, c'est leur terre, ils respectent. Mais les colons vietnamiens d'aujourd'hui, ceux qui envahissent toutes ces zones… La vallée de Dran, où il y avait oh trois ou quatre mille montagnards, du jour au lendemain, 300.000 Vietnamiens, oui ! J'ai des chiffres, j'ai tout, j'ai des documents. En pays conquis. Ce n'est pas leur terre, ils détruisent tout, rendement rendement rendement. Et maintenant la terre est usée, il n'y a plus rien, ils crèvent de faim, boat people, et voilà ! Trop pressés. Le vrai paysan n'est jamais pressé. On ne tire pas sur une plante pour qu'elle pousse, on attend. Simple comme bonjour. Et ça explique les boat people. Il y a aucune raison politique, aucune aucune aucune. Parce qu'ils se foutaient éperdument du Marxisme – je parle des gens de Hanoi. Ils s'en sont servis pour avoir l'aide russe, le matériel, pour avoir des slogans, la langue de bois et cetera, mais c'était le nationalisme, le patriotique et tout ce qu'on veut, récupéré.

Sur les plateaux, ce n'était pas chez eux. Ils ont tellement détruit la forêt. Parce qu'un Vietnamien ne supporte pas un arbre. Il a la haine des arbres. Le Vietnamien, c'est un maraîcher, riziculteur et maraîcher ; table rase, tout est tout propre, tout net.

AH – Et [dans] les deltas il n'y a pas d'arbres.

JD – Nulle part ! Nulle part, en pays vietnamien. Ils ne peuvent pas supporter un arbre. S'il y en a un, ils l'abattent. Le rendement, le rendement à toute vitesse. C'est vietnamien, parce que ce sont des riziculteurs, les pieds dans l'eau, et des maraîchers. Il faut que ça rende le plus possible, alors on s'arrange pour que tout soit comme une rizière et ils ont tellement bien fait que 90 millions de Vietnamiens crèvent de faim. Il y a quelques ans, ils essayaient de foutre le camp, parce qu'ils n'en pouvaient plus de crever. Il n'y a pas de raison politique là-dedans. Ils ont usé, vidé, nettoyé leur pays. Comme les Russes, comme les Russes, ils ressemblent beaucoup aux Russes.

Je sais que tout le monde ne peut pas vivre au régime de l'essartage. C'est un régime de luxe pour une densité de huit à neuf au kilomètre carré.

Aux grandes densités, ce n'est pas possible. [Mais] entre l'essartage de luxe et la désertification, il y a peut-être une solution, hein ? Et en France, c'est ce qu'on est en train de faire. La désertification de la culture, dans tous les sens du mot.

AH – Est-ce qu'en France on fait comme en Angleterre, où les agriculteurs sont payés pour ne pas cultiver leurs champs ?

JD – Ouais. Ici, à côté, il y a des vignerons qui ont été payés pour arracher leurs vignes. C'est typique, il y a des vignes arrachées sur le chemin. Le désert partout sur la terre.

Moi j'ai une autre conception de l'économie, puis voilà ! Elle n'est pas folle ma conception.

Bon, maintenant vous allez faire dodo, vous êtes crevé.

[Pause : reprise le lendemain matin.]

Vous avez rêvé cette nuit ?

AH – Je n'en suis pas conscient.

JD – Parce que tout le monde rêve, même les chiens. Oui, endormis, puis *biyiiii*, un cauchemar. Ils voyaient des choses intérieurement, ils entendaient des sons. Moi, depuis longtemps, j'ai pris l'habitude de la technique de mémorisation des rêves au fur et à mesure. Et les plus intéressants je les note. J'en ai fait une dizaine de cahiers parce qu'il y en a eu de très intéressants. C'est très important pour se connaître.

Les rêves, je les ai étudiés là-bas. Bon, il y a des sons, il y a des couleurs, on rêve en couleur. Et il y a des rêves quelquefois qui les inquiètent et pour s'en débarrasser il faut qu'ils les racontent à quelqu'un, très intime. Surtout chez les Jörai, j'avais des femmes qui venaient me raconter leurs rêves le matin. Pas un ethnologue qui a eu une chance pareille ! Elles me racontent, comme ça ça les débarrasse, il n'y a pas d'effets mauvais et c'est moi qui ramasse tout. Théoriquement pour elles j'étais plus fort, je pouvais ramasser tout ça et puis elles étaient libres. Il y a un tas de choses là-dedans.

AH – Comment ils sont, ces rêves ?

JD – Il ne faut jamais interpréter, il faut les prendre comme ça. C'est comme un morceau de musique, faut pas dire que ça signifie telle chose, on l'écoute, ça produit un certain effet et c'est tout. Il ne faut pas interpréter comme un tableau. On reçoit, voilà.

Le rêve c'est toujours extrêmement court. J'ai des bouquins de récits de rêves, des gens qui font une page pour une petite histoire qui a duré un quart de second. Pour mémoriser ça, il faut prendre un mot clé ou une image clé, ou une couleur ou quelque chose que vous attrapez et au réveil vous fixez sur le mot clé, tout le rêve revient. Ça se tient en trois lignes, tellement bref... Plus de la moitié des possibilités de notre cerveau fonctionnent à l'état de rêve. À l'état de veille nous n'utilisons que très peu de nos possibilités. Les gens qui s'imaginent peu doués, sans imagination, banals, quand ils se mettent à faire attention à leurs rêves, ils s'aperçoivent qu'ils ont des richesses fantastiques, de l'imagination débordante. Souvent c'est la culture du milieu familial ou autre chose qui bloque.

C'est comme pour la langue. Vous savez que les petits enfants du monde entier, les bébés, arrivent à prononcer toutes les choses qui sont prononçables dans le monde. Il y a un cas particulier que j'ai étudié : c'est la glottalisée, les consonnes glottalisées « 'bo 'be 'de ». Très peu d'Européens peuvent les prononcer, très peu. Les Vietnamiens n'en ont que deux, 'be et 'de. C'est pour ça ils vous disent « 'bonjour » et non pas « bonjour ». Le « b » implosif : « 'bon, 'bonjour ». Et j'ai entendu des petits enfants français, des bébés de deux ans par là, faire des glottalisées magnifiques. L'éducation, le fait d'entendre la langue des parents, ça limite, ça limite, ça limite de plus en plus les moyens d'expression pour se faire comprendre. Il y a eu des possibilités énormes. L'éducation les met sur des rails, il ne reste plus grande chose.

Parce que ce que je vous dis sur la langue c'est comme ce que je vous disais sur le rêve. Il y a un point commun là-dedans : c'est le cerveau. Le cerveau qui commande le langage. À la naissance les cerveaux sont capables d'un tas de choses. Même avant. C'est pour ça que c'est très important qu'une femme enceinte entende de belles choses, même de la musique. Oui très important pour l'enfant dans le ventre de la mère. Il y a des mères qui font ça très bien, elles parlent et ça reste. Il y a de la mémoire de ce qui s'était passé avant la sortie du ventre. Ça existe la mémoire de l'état fœtal.

[*Au chien :*] Chien ! Coucher ! Mais non je te dis.

Les chasseurs, vous entendez de l'autre côté ? Grrrr je déteste les chasseurs, comme toutes les armes. Puis un de ces jours ils vont tirer sur mes chiens. C'est pour ça je fais très attention, surtout le samedi et le dimanche. Ils tirent sur n'importe quoi. Il n'y a rien, quelques petits lapins dans les vignes, c'est tout. Ils tirent sur ce qu'ils peuvent. Pour le plaisir de tuer.

[*Au chien :*] Là tu vas aller dehors ! Je te garantis ! Sors !

Si tu dis « dors », il comprend. Une phrase, il ne comprend pas. Là, je ne sais plus qui me disait que l'anglais est très utile pour parler aux chiens parce que c'est monosyllabique. « *Down* ! » c'est beaucoup mieux que « assis ! » ou « couché ! » ou autre chose. Un seul son. Langue de chien, l'anglais.

[*Pause*]

AH – Est-ce qu'ils se racontent les rêves ?

JD – Entre eux ? Dans la vie courante je vous ai dit non, habituellement pas, c'est pour s'en débarrasser, mais à une personne seulement. Mais dans la mythologie, dans la littérature orale, oui. Il y a le héros, qui est jeune homme, qui a un copain, qui raconte, qui a vu en rêve une belle jeune fille, qu'il lui prenait des seins, et cetera et cetera. Alors les autres lui disent, « fais nous rencontrer ta belle, hein ! » et cetera. Voilà le genre qui peut se produire en littérature. On raconte pour que ça entraîne l'histoire.

AH – Technique littéraire plutôt qu'autre chose ?

JD – Oui mais on ne peut pas distinguer le littéraire du courant pas plus qu'on peut distinguer le sacré du profane. Chez eux, tout a un caractère sacré et chez eux tout a un caractère littéraire. Ce sont des littéraires, ces paysans, ces sauvages… ce sont des littéraires ! Dans la conversation courante, ils s'arrangent pour faire des assonances, des allitérations, des rimes. Ils ne peuvent pas s'empêcher. Ce sont des maîtres de la parole, c'est extraordinaire. J'ai des milliers de pages de textes enregistrés puis transcrits, pas tous traduits encore, c'est délirant. Et tout le monde aime ça, les jeunes comme les vieux. Alors c'est bien simple, à l'école ils sont nuls en math, ils sont très forts en lettres. L'inverse des Vietnamiens qui sont des matheux, des ingénieurs, des industriels et qui ne sont pas très forts en lettres et en philo. Ils n'ont pas de littérature les Vietnamiens, presque pas, rien d'intéressant. C'est juste l'inverse.

AH – Et les contes, ça se raconte comment chez les Jörai ?

JD – Ça dépend de l'âge. Les jeunes qui commencent à s'exercer racontent n'importe quoi, n'importe quand, n'importe comment, à n'importe qui. C'est facile pour l'étranger qui débarque, qui sait un petit peu la langue et qui commence avec les gosses. On apprend beaucoup de choses déjà. On sait qu'il y a une histoire, qu'il y a un type qui a un nom d'héros et puis au bout de quelques années quand on se débrouille mieux dans la langue, on arrive à trouver quelqu'un qui vous raconte ça pendant quatre ou cinq heures de suite. Parce que le gosse, ça dure dix minutes. C'est comme *Cendrillon* ou *Le Petit Chaperon rouge*. Vous demandez à un gosse de vous le raconter, ça durera trois minutes. S'il y a encore quelques vieux conteurs, vieilles conteuses en France, ils vous racontent ça pendant des heures.

Ce n'est pas du tout la même circonstance. Pour l'enfant il n'y a pas de circonstance. Pour le conteur il doit y avoir des époques de l'année, des époques où il n'y a pas de travail à la rizière et quand il pleut. Et le soir, la nuit, dans leur maison, la maison du voisin, ou des copains chez qui on va passer la soirée. Puis si ça leur prend envie – il n'est pas question de leur demander – ils font un conte. Ça peut durer une heure, ça peut durer cinq heures, jusqu'à l'aube… Et vous avez ça dans tout le Sud-est asiatique. Le reste du monde je n'ai pas étudié.

Il n'y a pas de rite particulier. Il y a simplement une époque de l'année, une heure de la journée, en fonction de la liberté, de moins de travaux, [ou] qu'on puisse veiller un peu plus tard. Parce que vous savez, quand vous travaillez dans la rizière, c'est à sept heures et demi on va se coucher. Quand on ne fiche rien de toute sa journée, parce qu'il pleut trop ou parce que le riz vient d'être moissonné tout simplement, il n'y a plus rien à faire.

C'est la meilleure époque, de mi-décembre à fin janvier. Alors ils n'ont rien à ficher. Les travaux de réfection de la maison, ça se fait plutôt à partir de février. La préparation des champs se fait en mars-avril. Alors là, à la fin de l'année, décembre-janvier, c'est plus facile d'entendre des contes. C'est spontané. Ils sont vraiment bordéliques, s'ils ont envie, ils racontent, c'est tout.

AH – Il n'y a pas de conteurs professionnels ?

JD – Non, pas professionnels. Non, ce n'est pas du tout comme en Afrique avec le griot. Non, ils ne se font pas payer. Ils le font pour le plaisir. Ils ne boivent pas, jamais avant de conter, ils boivent après. Ce n'est pas de l'alcool, c'est la bière de riz. Il faut distinguer l'alcool qui est distillé, de la bière qui est faite avec du grain et du vin qui est fait avec des fruits. On fait du vin de banane et on fait de la bière de riz ou de maïs. Alors, ils ne boivent qu'après, jamais avant de conter ça abîme la voix. Et comme, vous savez, ils ne sont pas très sobres, quand ils boivent ils boivent trop, ils ne peuvent plus raconter. Ils le savent très bien.

AH – Et ils content uniquement avec la voix ?

JD – Il n'y a pas de musique. Beaucoup sont aussi musiciens, tout le monde est musicien. Presque tout le monde a un instrument de musique qu'il fabrique lui-même. Ceux qu'ils fabriquent eux-mêmes sont des vents et des cordes, genre flûte, pipeau et genre cithare. Presque tous jouent aussi d'un instrument mais il n'y a jamais d'accompagnement avec le conte. Il n'y a pas de gestes, ils sont assis.

AH – Beaucoup de gens ?

JD – Oh non, une dizaine de personnes dans la case. Non, on ne fait pas de rassemblement pour ça. Compte tenu que c'est imprévisible, on ne sait pas quand il va conter. J'avais des amis, là dans le village, qui disaient « il y a un tel qui est conteur, qui va passer la soirée chez nous, il va peut-être conter, je n'en sais rien ». Il y a quelques uns qui sont venus conter chez moi pour me faire plaisir, tout seul.

AH – Pouvez-vous me donner un exemple d'un conte ?

JD – Beaucoup… J'ai appris à être conteur.

À Cerisy, je ne sais pas si vous connaissez les colloques de Cerisy, c'est un château en Normandie qui a un centre culturel où chaque été il y a une dizaine de colloques sur des sujets très précis. J'avais été invité – il y a sept ou huit ans au moins – pour un colloque sur le mythe et la mythologie. J'ai fait une conférence et j'avais demandé, dans ce très grand hall du château, d'avoir la possibilité de conter le soir. Alors on avait préparé le grenier du château, une vraie cathédrale, une splendeur ! Une cinquantaine de personnes… je me suis mis à conter. J'avais demandé qu'on nous serve des boissons. Une très bonne organisation. C'est très sympathique : on nous servait des punchs, des trucs comme ça. J'ai conté un tas d'histoires, ça a commencé vers dix heures du soir à peu près, juste après le dîner. À minuit ils n'en pouvaient plus et ils m'en demandaient encore. Et de mémoire ! Je n'avais aucun texte, j'avais rien apporté, je ne pensais pas du tout conter. Je pensais faire ma conférence. Je l'avais dans la tête, la conférence, et puis c'est tout. Et quand je me suis dit « mais ils aimeraient peut-être que je conte ? », je me suis promené dans le parc du château toute la journée avant cette soirée-là, pour me remémorer, sans aucune note, sans rien, pour me remémorer de jolies histoires. Puis hop, c'est parti !

Works of Jacques Dournes

For a more complete bibliography, see Laurent Dartigues and Pierre Le Roux, "Jacques Dournes, son oeuvre. Une nouvelle bibliographie," *Moussons* 3, 2001: 113–27.

Dournes, Jacques. "Structure sociale des montagnards du Haut-Donnai. Tribu des riziculteurs." *Bulletin de la Société des Études Indochinoises* 24-2 (1948): 101–6.

———. "Chants antiques de la montagne." *Bulletin de la Société des Études Indochinoises* 24-3 (1948): 9–111.

———. "L'âme et les songes. Étude Moï pour servir à la philosophie des primitifs." *France-Asie* 55 (1949): 1107–23.

———. *Dictionnaire Sre (Koho)-Francais.* Saigon: Imprimerie d'Extrême-Orient, 1950.

Dam Bo (Jacques Dournes). "Les populations montagnardes du Sud-Indochinois." *France-Asie* 49–50 (numéro spécial, 1950).

Dournes, Jacques. "Nri (Coutumier Srê; extraits)." *France-Asie* 60 (1951): 1232–41.

———. "Le chant et l'écriture." *France-Asie* 73 (1952): 229–34.

———. "Fêtes saisonnières des Srê." *Bulletin de l'École française d'Extrême-Orient* 46 (1954): 599–609.

———. *En suivant la piste des hommes sur les Hauts-Plateaux du Viêt-Nam.* Paris: Julliard, 1955.

———. "Les racines d'un art missionnaire." *Art Sacré* 1-2 (Sept.–Oct.), 1962.

———. *Dieu aime les païens. Une mission de l'église sur les plateaux du Viêt-Nam.* Paris: Montaigne, 1963.

———. *Le Père m'a envoyé. Réflexions à partir d'une situation missionnaire.* Paris: Cerf, 1965.

———. *L'Offrande des Peuples. Recherches et remarques sur le binome activité—action liturgique.* Paris: Cerf, 1967.

———. *L'homme et son mythe.* Paris: Aubier-Montaigne, 1968.

———. *Au plus près du loin. Projet pour la Mission.* Paris: Ed. Montaigne, 1969.

———. *Bois-bambou : aspect végétal de l'univers Jörai.* Paris: Éditions du CNRS, 1969.

———. "Recherches sur le Haut-Champa." *France-Asie* 24-2 (1970): 143–62.

———. *Coordonnées : structures Jörai familiales et sociales.* Paris: Institut d'Ethnologie, 1972.

————. "Pötao, les maîtres des états, étude d'anthropologie politique chez les Jörai." PhD dissertation, Sorbonne, Paris, 1973.

————. "Les marches sauvages : chez les minorités ethniques du Sud-Indochinois." *Les Temps Modernes,* 1975: 1552–82.

————. *Le parler des Jörai et le style de leur expression.* Paris: Publications orientalistes de France, 1976.

————. *Pötao, une théorie du pouvoir chez les Indochinois jörai.* Paris: Flammarion, 1977.

————. *Mythes srê. Trois pièces de littérature orale d'une ethnie austro-asiatique.* Paris: SELAF, 1977.

————. *Akhan: contes oraux de la forêt indochinoise.* Paris: Payot, 1977.

————. "Sam Bam, le Mage et le Blanc dans l'Indochine centrale des années trente." *L'Ethnographie* 76/1 (1978a): 85–108.

————. "The history of the natives of central Vietnam." In *Identités collectives et relations interculturelles,* edited by G. Michaud. Brussel: Editions Complexe, 1978b.

————. *Forêt femme folie. Une traversée de l'imaginaire Jörai.* Paris: Aubier, 1978c.

————. *Minorities of Central Vietnam: Autochthonous Indochinese Peoples.* London: Minority Rights Group, Report No. 18 (revised edition), 1980.

————. *Florilège jörai : contes populaires du Vietnam.* Paris: Sudestasie, 1987.

————. "The Spirit of Laws: A first presentation of data on the "customary laws" of the Indochinese Jorai people." *Contributions to Southeast Asian Ethnography* 7 (1988): 7–25.

————. "Sabre et bouclier de la guerre? Aspects des conflits tribaux principalement en pays Jörai." Unpublished manuscript, 1989.

————. *Florilège srê : contes populaires du Vietnam.* Paris: Sudestasie, 1990.

————. *Pays Jörai.* Hanoi: EFEO/Nxb Tri Thức. Forthcoming.

Bibliography

Baptiste, Pierre, and Thierry Zéphir, eds. *Trésors d'art du Vietnam, la sculpture du Champa, Ve–XVe siècles*. Paris: Éditions de la Réunion des musées nationaux, 2005.

Boulbet, Jean. *Pays des Maa', domaine des génies, Nggar Maa', Nggar Yaang : essai d'ethno-histoire d'une population proto-indochinoise du Viêt Nam central*. Paris: EFEO, 1967.

Bourotte, Bernard. "Essai d'histoire des populations montagnardes du Sud-Indochinois jusqu'à 1945." *BSEI* 30, 1 (1955): 17–100.

Coedès, Georges. *Les états hindouisés d'Indochine et d'Indonésie*. Paris: de Boccard, 1989 (first edition 1948).

Choron-Baix, Catherine. *L'homme des Jörai, Vidéo-portrait de Jacques Dournes*. Documentary, CNRS, 2005. http://www.iiac.cnrs.fr/cetsah/spip.php?article263 &lang=pt_br (consulted October 17, 2009).

Condominas, Georges. *Nous avons mangé la forêt de la pierre-génie Gôo*. Paris: Mercure de France, 1957.

Cupet, capitaine. "Voyages au Laos et chez les sauvages du Sud-Est de l'Indo-Chine." *Mission Pavie. Géographie et voyages. Vol. 3.* Paris: E. Leroux, 1900.

Dartigues, Laurent, and Pierre Le Roux. "Jacques Dournes, son oeuvre. Une nouvelle bibliographie." *Moussons* 3 (2001): 113–27.

Delvert, Jean. *Le paysan cambodgien*. Paris: Imprimerie nationale, 1961.

Dourisboure, Pierre. *Les sauvages Ba-Hnars (Cochinchine orientale), souvenirs d'un missionnaire*. Paris: D. de Soye, 1873.

Gay, Bernard. "Vue nouvelle sur la composition ethnique du Campa." In Lafont, ed., *Actes du séminaire sur le Campa*, 49–58.

Guérin, Mathieu, Andrew Hardy, Nguyễn Văn Chính, and Stan B.-H. Tan. *Des montagnards aux minorités ethniques. Quelle intégration nationale pour les habitants des hautes terres du Vietnam et du Cambodge ?* Paris-Bangkok: L'Harmattan-IRASEC, 2003.

Guy, John. "Artistic Exchange, Regional Dialogue and the Cham Territories." In Hardy, Cucarzi, and Zolese, eds, *Champa*, 127–54.

Hardy, Andrew. "Eaglewood and the Economic History of Champa and Central Vietnam." In Hardy, Cucarzi, and Zolese, eds, *Champa*, 107–26.

————. *Red Hills: Migrants and the State in the Highlands of Vietnam*. Copenhagen: NIAS Press, 2003.

Hardy, Andrew, Mauro Cucarzi, and Patrizia Zolese, eds. *Champa and the Archaeology of Mỹ Sơn (Vietnam)*. Singapore: NUS Press, 2009.

Hickey, Gerald C. *Sons of the Mountains, Ethnohistory of the Vietnamese Central Highlands to 1954*. New Haven and London: Yale University Press, 1982.

Jaspan, Mervyn A. *Recent Developments among the Cham of Indochina: The Revival of Champa*. Hull: Publications of the Centre for South-East Asian Studies, University of Hull, 1969.

Lafont, Pierre-Bernard, ed. *Actes du séminaire sur le Campa organisé à l'Université de Copenhague le 23 mai 1987*. Paris: Centre d'histoire et civilisations de la péninsule indochinoise, 1988.

————. *Le Campa, Géographie—Population—Histoire*. Paris: Les Indes savantes, 2007.

Lerat, Mary-Paule. "Jacques Dournes : ethnologue, missionnaire, colonisateur ?" *Sudestasie* 48–49 (1987): 67–71.

Lewis, Norman. *A Dragon Apparent: Travels in Cambodia, Laos, and Vietnam*. London: Jonathan Cape, 1951.

Mak Phoeun. "La communauté Cam au Cambodge du XVe au XIXe siècle, historique de son implantation et son rôle dans la vie politique khmère." In Lafont, ed, *Actes du séminaire sur le Campa*, 83–93.

Maitre, Henri. *Les jungles moï, Mission Henri Maitre (1909–1911), Indochine Sud-Centrale : exploration et histoire des hinterlands moï du Cambodge, de la Cochinchine, de l'Annam et du bas Laos*. Paris: Émile Larose, 1912. (Vietnamese Edition: *Rừng Người Thượng*, Hanoi: EFEO/Nxb Tri Thức, 2008.)

————. *Les régions moï du Sud Indo-Chinois, le plateau du Darlac*. Paris: Plon-Nourrit, 1909.

Mus, Paul. "Cultes indiennes et indigènes au Champa." *BEFEO* 33 (1933): 367–410.

Nakamura, Rie. "*Awar-Ahier*: Two Keys to Understanding the Cosmology and Ethnicity of the Cham People (Ninh Thuan Province, Vietnam)." In Hardy, Cucarzi, and Zolese, eds., *Champa*, 78–106.

Nguyễn Thị Kim Vân. "Hiện tượng Lịch sử—Văn hóa Pơtao Apui từ tư liệu đến thực địa" [The historical-cultural phenomenon of the Pơtao Apui, from documents to fieldwork]. In *Pơtao Apui, Tư liệu và Nhận định* [Pơtao Apui, Documents and Assessment]. Pleiku: Sở Văn hóa Thông tin Gia Lai, 2004: 15–37.

Nguyễn Tiến Đông. "Di tích Cát Tiên với Xứ Mạ" [The Cát Tiên site and the Mạ people's territory]. *Văn hóa Nghệ thuật*, 1 (2000): 25–27.

————. "Khu di tích Cát Tiên ở Lâm Đồng" [The Cát Tiên group of sites in Lâm Đồng]. PhD dissertation, Institute of Archaeology, Hanoi, 2001.

Nguyễn Văn Kự, Ngô Văn Doanh, and Andrew Hardy. *Peregrinations into Cham Culture*. Hanoi: EFEO/Nxb Thế Giới, 2005.

Parmentier, Henri. *Inventaire descriptif des monuments cams de l'Annam.* Vol. 2. Paris: Leroux, 1918.

———. *L'art architectural Hindou dans l'Inde et en Extrême-Orient.* Paris: Van Oest, 1948.

Peleggi, Maurizio. *Lords of Things: The Fashioning of the Siamese Monarchy's Modern Image.* Honolulu: Hawaii University Press, 2002.

Pelliot, Paul. "Le Fou-Nan." *BEFEO* 3, 2 (1903): 248–303.

Po Dharma. *Le Panduranga (Campa). 1802–1835: ses rapports avec le Vietnam.* Paris: EFEO, 1987.

Salemink, Oscar. *The Ethnography of Vietnam's Central Highlanders, A Historical Contextualisation, 1850–1990.* London and New York: RoutledgeCurzon, 2003.

Trần Kỳ Phương and Rie Nakamura. The Mỹ Sơn and Pô Nagar Nha Trang Sanctuaries: On the Cosmological Dualist Cult of the Champa Kingdom in Central Vietnam as Seen from Art and Anthropology. Singapore: Asia Research Institute Working Paper No. 10, 2008.

Trần Kỳ Phương and Vũ Hữu Minh. "Cửa Đại Chiêm (Port of Great Champa) in the 4th–15th centuries." In Ancient Town of Hội An, Hanoi: Foreign Languages Publishing House, 1991: 77–81.

Vickery, Michael. "Histoire du Champa." In Baptiste and Zéphir, eds., *Trésors d'art du Vietnam,* 23–35.

Woodside, Alexander B. *Vietnam and the Chinese Model: A Comparative Study of the Nguyen and Ching Civil Government in the First Half of the Nineteenth Century.* Cambridge, Mass.: Harvard University Press, 1971.

Index

Milton Keynes UK
Ingram Content Group UK Ltd.
UKHW011117070224
437385UK00001BA/28